The Pitti Palace

The Pitti Palace

THE PALACE AND ITS ART

Marilena Mosco

Introduction by Marco Chiarini

Philip Wilson

First published in 1997 by
Philip Wilson Publishers Limited
143-149 Great Portland Street
London W1N 5FB

Distributed in the USA and Canada by
Antique Collectors' Club Limited
Market Street Industrial Park
Wappingers' Falls
NY 12590
USA

ISBN   0 85667 469 9

Designed by Andrew Shoolbred
Translated from Italian by Heather Roberts
English translation edited by Lucinda Collinge
Printed and bound in Italy by
Società Editoriale Libraria per azioni, Trieste

The dimensions of all paintings and works of art are given
in centimetres, unless stated otherwise, and presented
as height x width.

Contents

Introduction

The severe, dramatically rusticated façade of Palazzo Pitti gives little indication of the treasures within. According to Giorgio Vasari, the original design of Luca Pitti's palace was by Filippo Brunelleschi, although construction of the building began in 1457, after his death. The interior of the Palace shows little trace from the fifteenth and sixteenth centuries, but reflects later styles, from Baroque to Neo-Classical. The great courtyard, with wings reaching towards the Boboli Garden, was designed by Bartolomeo Ammannati and added to the Palace in the latter part of the sixteenth century, at the time of Cosimo I de' Medici. It has remained virtually intact, except that the arcading of the upper floors was filled in, leaving only the ground floor as an open loggia. It is this courtyard that gives visual emphasis to the back of the Palace, directing the eye towards the garden built on the slopes of the Boboli hill, with its open-air theatre.

One of the most spectacular views of the garden and theatre is from the Statue Gallery, which leads into the oldest and most celebrated part of the Pitti, the Palatine Gallery, 'Palatina' meaning 'of the Palace'. Like the Palazzo, the gallery and its contents reflect the tastes of generations of collectors from the time of Cosimo I. Some treasures have remained in the gallery since the sixteenth century, while some are exhibited in other Florentine museums, from the Uffizi, the Bargello, and the Accademia, to the Archaeological Museum and the Museum of San Marco. As the home of five generations of Medici Grand Dukes and then of three generations of the Hapsburg-Lorraine family, the Pitti Palace was also the original home of many of the finest works in Florence. The collections of these rulers were the foundations of the Palatine Gallery, also known as the Pitti Gallery, in memory of the original owners of the Palace. Two of the most important collections of paintings formed by the Medici were those of Cardinal Leopoldo, the son of Cosimo II, and of Grand Prince Ferdinando, the son of Grand Duke Cosimo III. It was Cosimo III who began the systematic arrangement of the collection, enriching it with other

Pitti Palace: Exterior

pieces acquired by the Medici. Towards the end of the eighteenth century when the Lorraine decided to organise a proper gallery in the Palace, they chose the five rooms on the façade, previously used by the Medici Grand Dukes as winter apartments. These rooms had splendid Baroque fresco and plaster decorations by Pietro da Cortona, a scheme that was admired and imitated throughout Europe. Paintings for the gallery were selected from the vast collection in the palace and re-arranged in the seventeenth-century fashion, according to their size and framing, to create the most pleasing overall effect. Thus, masterpieces, many of them altarpieces, by the most admired artists of the sixteenth and seventeenth centuries, from Raphael and Titian, Andrea del Sarto, Fra Bartolomeo, Agnolo Bronzino, Paolo Veronese to Jacopo Tintoretto, alternate with the portraits that form a significant part of the collection. Raphael's portraits of Agnolo and Maddalena Doni (who commissioned Michelangelo's famous tondo of the Holy Family in the Uffizi) were added in 1825, and their simple Neo-Classical frames reflect the period of their acquisition. The paintings of the Venetian school, including some fine Titians, came to the Pitti Palace from Urbino as part of the dowry of the last member of the della Rovere family, Vittoria, at the time of her marriage to Ferdinando II de' Medici. Later, works by Peter Paul Rubens, Anthony Van Dyck and Diego Velazquez further enriched the collection, adding to the splendid range of portraits.

In the Sala di Prometeo, behind the main rooms overlooking the façade, are some beautiful paintings from the Early Renaissance in Florence: the *Bartolini Tondo* of the Virgin and Child by Fra Filippo Lippi, the *Death of Lucretia* by his son, Filippino Lippi, two portraits by Sandro Botticelli and a tondo by Luca Signorelli. Other paintings in the rooms at the back of the Palace include seventeenth-century genre paintings, landscapes by Gaspard Dughet, Jacob van Ruysdael, Cornelis van Poelenburgh, Paul Bril, and

View of the Pitti Palace from the Boboli Garden

Ludolph Backhuysen, as well as still-lifes by Rachel Ruysch and Willem van Aelst, which are suited to the more intimate rooms decorated in the Neo-Classical style.

From the end of the nineteenth century to the beginning of the twentieth there were many changes at the Pitti Palace, which was the official residence of the Italian royal family, the House of Savoy, when Florence was briefly the capital of Italy (1865-1871). In 1919, when the building came under the control of the Italian State, more exhibition space was made available and the collections were reorganized. It was only in the first half of this century that the Palatine Gallery, originally housing some five hundred paintings, expanded into the Volterrano wing (which takes its name from the painter who executed the lovely ceiling decoration in the mid-seventeenth century for Vittoria della Rovere). These rooms were used to exhibit Florentine paintings of the seventeenth century, mostly acquired by the Medici and stored but not displayed in the Uffizi. At the same time a large number of earlier masterpieces was passed from the Pitti Palace to the Uffizi. Both the Museo degli Argenti on the ground floor and the Galleria d'Arte Moderna on the second floor opened during this period. The Museo degli Argenti complements the paintings in the Palatine Gallery with a display of the Medici's rich collection of pietre dure (hardstone) vases, and of objects in silver, crystal, amber and ivory, together with jewels and goldsmiths' work from Salzburg, with cameos and reliefs in a variety of precious materials. The Galleria d'Arte Moderna displays mainly eighteenth- and nineteenth-century art, the last works acquired for the Pitti Palace under the Lorraine and the Savoy. It also documents the development of the Macchiaioli, Tuscan painters of the second half of the nineteenth century who, with the French Impressionists, signalled the end of academic painting.

Thus, the Pitti Palace offers riches in an abundance and variety rivalled by only a few great nineteenth-century museums (the Louvre in Paris, the Kunsthistorisches Museum in Vienna and the Metropolitan Museum in New York). The three ruling families of Tuscany, the Medici, the Lorraine and the Savoy, all lived here, and here, under frescoed ceilings and crystal chandeliers, their collections are displayed in a setting of almost unparalleled splendour.

Marco Chiarini

The Pitti Palace

IL PALAZZO PITTI

The Pitti Palace is the dominant element on Florence's 'left bank', linking the popular Oltrarno district and the Boboli hill crowned by the Belvedere Fortress. The Palace is also linked to the centre of the city across the river by the Vasari corridor, which crosses the Ponte Vecchio and passes through the Uffizi Gallery to the Palazzo Vecchio.

Although over a period of four hundred years the Palace housed three ruling dynasties, the Medici, the Lorraine and the Savoy, it has retained the name of its founder Luca Pitti (1393-1472), who was a friend and rival of Cosimo il Vecchio de' Medici. According to legend, Luca discovered a plot against Cosimo and was rewarded with the plans for the Palace, which Cosimo had commissioned from the architect Filippo Brunelleschi but rejected as 'too princely'. The building was begun in 1457, after Brunelleschi's death, by his pupil Luca Fancelli, who retained the original design: a square structure with seven windows and three doorways on the façade, built of rusticated stone quarried from the Boboli hill (see the detail in *Portrait of a Woman* by an anonymous fifteenth-century artist in the Museo degli Argenti).

The Palace was unfinished at the time of Luca's death in 1472, and work remained suspended until 1550 when the building and the Boboli hill were bought by Eleanor of Toledo, wife of Cosimo I de' Medici. The family was eager to acquire a more spacious and salubrious home than the dark, confined quarters of the Palazzo di Piazza (della Signoria) in the city centre, which then became known as the Palazzo Vecchio. To convert the Pitti into a palace worthy of the newly created Grand Duke of Tuscany, Cosimo chose the sculptor and architect Bartolomeo Ammannati. A follower of Jacopo Sansovino and Michelangelo who had already built the fountain in the Piazza della Signoria and the beautiful Ponte Santa Trìnita, Ammannati designed a monumental courtyard for the rear of the Palace, built from the same rusticated stone as the façade. The original courtyard, altered in the seventeenth and eighteenth centuries, had open loggias on three storeys, which gave a more dramatic and picturesque effect than the present one with the arcading limited to the ground floor. Nevertheless, the rear of the Palace, seen from the Boboli Garden, is more pleasantly impressive than the very severe front

The Neptune Fountain (detail), Boboli Garden

façade, which one writer likened to a prison fortress.

The shady Moses Grotto, at the end of the courtyard, serves as a link between the walled courtyard and the natural realm of the gardens. The grotto was decorated at the height of the seventeenth century with allegorical statues inside and figures of Hercules without, alluding to the triumph of Law and Government under the Grand Duke Ferdinando II. From the sixteenth century it provided the backdrop for many spectacular entertainments and naval battles staged in the courtyard. The Artichoke Fountain on the terrace above, designed by Francesco Susini, also played an important part in dramatic performances, and as late as 1937 was part of the set for a performance of Claudio Monteverdi's opera, the Coronation of Poppea. Over the centuries the Palace was gradually enlarged, but with the Florentines' respect for tradition the additions were always in keeping with the original Brunelleschi plan. Under the Grand Dukes Cosimo II and Ferdinando II, in 1620 and 1640, Giulio and Alfonso Parigi added first three and then five windows to either side of the original façade.

In the eighteenth century, when the House of Lorraine succeeded the Medici as rulers of Tuscany, the palace was enlarged to the boundaries of the piazza with the wing of the Rondò di Mezzogiorno, or delle Carrozze, on the south side, for carriages, finished by the architect Giuseppe Ruggeri in 1783, and the Rondò di Settentrione, to the north, also known as di Bacco, begun by Giuseppe Maria Paoletti in 1784 and finished in 1815 by Pasquale Poccianti with the Rondò Sud.

Paoletti and Poccianti were also responsible for the Meridiana wing built on the south side of the main building, facing the Boboli Garden. This was the residence of Napoleon's sister Elisa Baciocchi in the early nineteenth century and of various members of the Savoy family until the early years of this century. Since 1983 it has housed the Costume Gallery.

The last addition to the Palace, on the north side of the building facing the Rondò di Bacco, is the great staircase and atrium built in 1896 for Umberto I, still in the style of Brunelleschi, as a grand entrance to the Palatine Gallery. This is now the exit and, like a magic circle, it completes the history of the Palace designed by the great Renaissance architect for Luca Pitti.

The Pitti Palace and the Boboli Garden

The Boboli Garden
IL GIARDINO DI BOBOLI

In 1457 an area referred to as Boboli is recorded in Luca Pitti's purchase of land for the 'garden with vines and fruit trees' mentioned in later documents. When the land was sold to Eleanor of Toledo it was called the 'vegetable garden of the Pitti', and the sculptor Niccolò Tribolo was employed to make it into something far grander, planting oak, bay, juniper and chestnut trees, most from the nurseries of the Medici Villa at Castello.

In 1553 the first grotto, the Grotticina di Madama, was built for Eleanor of Toledo, whose coat of arms, with that of the Medici, is visible above the entrance. The Grotto delle Capre, with three goats sculpted by Baccio Bandinelli and Giovanni di Paolo Fancelli, is typical of the Mannerist taste for the fantastic and bizarre, with stalactites and sponge stones surrounding the ceiling frescoes of putti and grotesques, attributed to Francesco Ubertini, known as Bachiacca.

The fountain with the statue of *Nano Morgante*, called *Bacchus*, by Valerio Cioli was built in 1560 near the Buontalenti Grotto. The grotto, which was commissioned from Bernardo Buontalenti by Francesco I de' Medici in 1583, consists of three interconnecting rooms decorated with sponge stone. The walls of the first room are covered with figures modelled by Piero Mati, after Buontalenti's design, apparently illustrating the myth of Deucalion and Pyrrha. In an opening in the ceiling there was once a large glass basin containing fish, now lost, but the frescoes by Bernardino Poccetti of satyrs and animals inspired by the Boboli menagerie still survive. The naturalistic effect was originally stronger with vegetation covering the walls and water playing over the surfaces, like the water features that delighted the Grand Duke Francesco I at the Medici Villa at Pratolino.

The decoration of the grotto was also rich in symbolism alluding to man's struggle to free himself from matter (copies of Michelangelo's *Prisoners*, originals in the Accademia) and from instinct (the statue of *Paris and Helen* by Vincenzo de' Rossi, 1587) before attaining beauty incarnate, the *Venus* by Giambologna (in the third room). Similarly, in the mosaic niches the 'mountains of crystal' in the form of dazzling flames symbolize fire which, with water, air and earth represent in miscrocosm the world of Renaissance man (like the Studiolo of Francesco I in the Palazzo Vecchio).

The Isolotto

View of the Boboli Garden and the amphitheatre

The Boboli Garden, with its grottoes and statues, was typical of the Italian gardens that were copied throughout Europe, as in the Luxembourg Gardens in Paris. Francesco Susini's Artichoke Fountain, built in 1642, is a triumphant display of tritons, putti, shells and cartouches in keeping with the spectacular amphitheatre built from 1630 by Giulio and Alfonso Parigi. This was the setting for magnificent entertainments like the Carosello, inspired by Torquato Tasso's Gerusalemme Liberata, which was held to celebrate the marriage of Ferdinando II to Vittoria della Rovere in 1634, and Il Mondo Trionfante, an equestrian ballet performed as part of the wedding celebrations of Cosimo III and Marguerite Louise d'Orléans in 1661.

During the seventeenth century, other statues, including the *Neptune* by Stoldo Lorenzi and *Abundance* by Giambologna (completed by Pietro Tacca), were installed at the top of the garden. A garden was also built on the hill behind the palace, around the *Monkey Fountain* attributed to Tacca and the Palazzina, which replaced a small villa used by Cardinal Leopoldo and later Gian Gastone de' Medici and which now houses the Porcelain Museum.

The most important work in the seventeenth century was the landscaping of the slope from the top of the Boboli towards Porta Romana. The central feature was a wide walk, the Viottolone, leading down to a large circular pond. From a small island at the centre of the pond, the Isolotto, rose Giambologna's great statue of *Oceanus* (now in the Bargello and replaced by a copy), surrounded by statues of *Perseus* and *Andromeda* and putti and the monstrous *Harpies* designed by Alfonso Parigi.

The majority of statues in the gardens are copies of ancient Roman sculpture, such as the two *Tyrannicides* (tyrant slayers) along the Viottolone, but there are also some important seventeenth-century works including the *Seasons* by Giovanni Caccini, also along the Viottolone, the two *Vendemmiatori* (harvesters) and the *Contadino che zappa* (hoeing peasant) by Valerio Cioli, near the Limonaia, the glasshouse where citrus trees are kept in winter.

The elegant Limonaia, which was built in 1776 on the site of the old Medici menagerie, was commissioned by the Grand Duke Peter Leopold of Lorraine from Zanobi Rosso, who was also responsible for the Caffehaus (coffee house), just below the Belvedere Fortress.

It was also Peter Leopold who opened the Boboli Garden to the public in 1766. He extended the garden with the semi-circular Prato delle Colonne, decorated with antique statues and busts, arranged for two porphyry statues of *Dacian Prisoners* from the Villa Medici to be placed at the entrance to the road leading to the Rondò di Bacco and placed the Egyptian Obelisk at the centre of the amphitheatre in 1790.

During the rule of the Savoy, the slope facing the Meridiana wing was covered in grass and the statue of the winged horse *Pegasus* sculpted by Aristodemo Costoli in 1865 was installed. In the twentieth century, when the Palace and the garden came under the control of the Italian State, many important theatrical events took place in the park, including performances of A Midsummer's Night Dream, As You Like It, Troilus and Cressida, Eurydice and the Coronation of Poppea. The Triumphs by Petrarch was the last entertainment held in the garden, which in 1990 became part of the museum complex, as an historical garden and open-air sculpture museum.

The Viottolone

The Grand Ducal Treasures

IL MUSEO DEGLI ARGENTI

The Museo degli Argenti has been described as 'the most fabulous Wunderkammer or chamber of marvels in Europe, with its amazing precious objects like a microcosm dissected in infinite detail and re-assembled in a symbolic unity for the contemplation of the powerful' (Mottola Molfino). The museum includes objets d'art from the former Gem Cabinet in the Uffizi, the ivory, amber and glass collections from the Bargello, the jewellery of the Electress Palatine (the very last of the Medici), and the treasury of the Salzburg princes, brought to Florence by Ferdinand III of Lorraine in 1814. It was this treasury of silver, exhibited in 1866 in the Salone di Giovanni da San Giovanni, which gave the museum its name. Opened in the 1920s, the Museo degli Argenti was renovated in the 1970s to display to best advantage both the precious objects and the splendid living quarters of the Grand Dukes.

In the antechamber of the museum are two Medici portraits and a genealogical tree, showing the various members of the family that have collected this extraordinary miscellany of objects: from the vases of Lorenzo the Magnificent (such as the one in red jasper, illustrated), to the cameos of Cosimo I (including one showing the Piazza della Signoria), the crystals of Francesco I, the pietre dure of Ferdinando I, the ambers of Maria Maddalena of Austria, the ivories of Leopoldo, and the jewellery of Anna Maria Luisa (the Electress Palatine who bequeathed to the city of Florence all the Medici treasures "as an ornament to the State, for the public benefit and to attract the curiosity of visitors".

In the time of the Medici, the SALONE DI GIOVANNI DA SAN GIOVANNI, one of the great state rooms along the façade, was used for receptions and banquets. The room takes its name from the painter of the frescoes on the long wall, executed in 1634 for the marriage of Ferdinando II de' Medici and Vittoria della Rovere, which is symbolised on the ceiling. With typically Florentine wit, Giovanni's frescoes depict Greek culture leaving Athens following the conquest of the Turks – represented by Greek books and philosphers driven from Mount Parnassus – and arriving in Florence, the new Athens, under the benevolent rule of Lorenzo the Magnificent. The frescoes that follow, by

Salone di Giovanni da San Giovanni

Francesco Furini, Cecco Bravo and Ottavio Vannini, show Lorenzo receiving the Muses, speaking to Prudence while the god of War flies away, receiving artists (including Michelangelo), presiding over the Platonic Academy in the Villa at Careggi, and dying, his memory represented by a medal saved by the swan and a bay tree planted as a symbol of fame.

The adjacent room, to the left of the entrance, has the death-mask and a portrait of Lorenzo the Magnificent, as well as his extraordinary collection of antique vases, mostly Roman or Byzantine, which he had mounted by fifteenth-century Florentine goldsmiths. His initials appear on the mounts. The vases themselves are of pietre dure, or hard stones, such as sardonyx, jasper, amethyst, agate, and the hardest of all, porphyry, which was also used for statues.

In the GROTTICINA, the dressing-room of the Grand Duchesses, there is a 'commesso di pietre tenere' floor, some small marble putti and a virtuoso wood carving, an *Allegory of the Arts and of Friendship between Princes*, by the English sculptor Grinling Gibbons, given by Charles II to Cosimo III in 1682.

Crossing the Salone di Giovanni da San Giovanni and passing the small private chapel, with seventeenth-century reliquaries, we come to the Sale di Rappresentanza (delegation rooms), part of the summer apartments of the Medici Grand Duke.

The SALA DELL'UDIENZA (audience chamber), where the Grand Duke received his official guests, was frescoed between 1636 and 1644 by the Bolognese painters Agostino Mitelli and Angelo Michele Colonna like a theatre backdrop, with small scenes illustrating the life of the palace. In the middle of the room is the Stipo di Alemagna, an ebony cabinet inlaid with panels of pietre dure made in Augsburg and given by Leopold, Archduke of the Tyrol, to his brother-in-law Ferdinando II de' Medici. The prie-dieu between the two windows was made for the Grand Duchess Maria Maddalena of Austria, the wife of Cosimo II. Note the mosaic panel and the flowers in pietre dure work on the base of the prie-dieu.

Vase in red jasper with two handles and a cover, made in Venice and mounted by Florentine goldsmiths in silver-gilt and enamel
Height 27 cm
Inv.no.638

Inscribed LAUR:MED, the vase was part of a collection belonging to Lorenzo de' Medici and perhaps to his father Piero. The vases were taken to Rome by Clement VII and converted into reliquaries by Leo X. After their return to Florence, they were displayed in a case designed by Michelangelo in San Lorenzo. In 1875 they were moved to the Uffizi and in 1925 to the Museo degli Argenti.

Audience chamber: Frescoes by Angelo Michele Colonna and Agostino Mitelli (Bologna 17th century)

Cabinet belonging to the Elector Palatine in ebony, gilt-bronze, mother-of-pearl and pietre dure. Designed by Giovan Battista Foggini, Florence 1709

280 x 162 x 54 cm
Inv. O.A. 909.

The central niche of this elaborate cabinet displays a figure of the Elector Palatine, the son-in-law of Grand Duke Cosimo III

The SALA DELL' UDIENZA PRIVATA (private audience chamber) was also frescoed by Mitelli and Colonna with illusionistic decoration showing figures from the court, including a young man with a telescope (an allusion to the contemporary discoveries of Galileo). The ceiling represents the *Apotheosis of Alexander the Great* with the Medici and della Rovere arms on either side. The room contains several tables in pietre dure, masterpieces of this traditional Florentine technique, which is still practiced today. Other fine examples can be seen in the renovated Museo dell'Opificio delle Pietre Dure (museum of the pietre dure works) in the centre of town.

The fresco decoration in the third SALA DELL' UDIENZA includes portraits of all the Medici family connected with the history of the Pitti Palace, and between the two doors stands the magnificent Stipo dell'Eletore Palatino (cabinet of the Elector Palatine), made in 1709 in Florence after the design of the court sculptor Giovan Battista Foggini. A wedding gift from the Grand Duke Cosimo III to his daughter Anna Maria Luisa on her marriage in Düsseldorf to the Elector Palatine, it was returned to Florence when she was widowed.

In the centre of the room is a large table made from a Roman porphyry wheel, while on the Boboli side stands a marble table with a fine wooden support with two harpies, attributed to the Florentine sculptor Dionigi Nigetti, active in the mid-sixteenth century, and commissioned by Cosimo I. The room also contains a reliquary in the form of a small circular temple with saints, made in the Grand Ducal workshops in the eighteenth century, and a remarkable *Deposition with the Virgin and Angels* by Massimiliano Soldani Bensi, a goldsmith and sculptor who worked for Cosimo III in the late seventeenth century.

Leaving the rooms running along the façade, we enter those on the side of the gardens, whose private character is indicated by their smaller dimensions. The SALA DEGLI AVORI (ivory room) contains valuable ivory vases and statues collected by Cardinal Leopoldo de' Medici in the seventeenth century. In a glass case to the right of the entrance there are turned ivory vases made between 1610 and 1631 by Marcus Heiden and Johann Eisenberg for the Prince of Coburg, and plundered by Prince Mattias de' Medici during the Thirty Years' War.

In the case to the left of the entrance is a series of putti in high relief inspired by the Flemish sculptor François Duquesnoy, and in the middle of the room is the virtuoso sculpture group showing the Roman hero *Marcus Curtius Leaping into the Chasm* by the Master of the Furies, a German artist active in the mid seventeenth century. In another glass case are ivory medallions, including one of *Cosimo III*, by Philip Sengher, the celebrated German ivory-turner who taught the art to the Grand Duke's eldest son, the Grand Prince Ferdinando (a small vase exhibited here is an example of his work). Another medallion is a portrait of Ferdinando's wife, the *Grand Duchess Violante of Bavaria*, made on the occasion of their marriage by another German ivory-turner, Balthasar Permoser. The table and inlaid wooden cabinet are the work of Leonard van der Vinne, famous for the intarsia work so much in demand in the Low Countries in the seventeenth and eighteenth centuries. The other two tables are by the seventeenth-century cabinetmaker Riccardo Bruni.

The second SALA DEGLI AVORI E DEI RELIQUIARI (ivory and reliquaries room) has objects commissioned by Cardinal Leopoldo, including small sculptures by Balthasar Stockamer showing classical subjects like *Bacchus, Venus and Cupid* and *Apollo*, as well as Christian subjects like the *Crucifixion*. Also of interest are the ebony box with an ivory dog belonging to the Grand Duchess Maria Maddalena of Austria, and the two concentric globes in wood and ivory with miniature portraits of Duke Wilhelm V of Bavaria and his family.

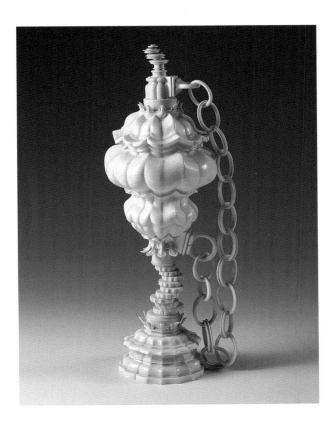

Johann Eisenberg. Ivory vase with a chain, 1626

Height 51.5 cm
Inv. Bargello n.54

This vase together with the other 26 in turned ivory were made in Coburg, Germany for the Duke of Saxony who was himself an amateur carver. In 1632, during the siege of Coburg, the vases were taken as booty by Prince Mattias de' Medici and brought to Florence.

Ebony box with an ivory dog

Dog, height 6 cm, length 18 cm
Box, 25 x 15 cm
Inv. A.S.E no. 187

This ivory belonged to Maria Maddalena of Austria in memory of her King Charles spaniel, given to her by Cosimo II. The breed became popular after being the favourite of Charles II of England.

The SALA DELLE AMBRE (amber room) was the bed-room of the last scion of the house of Medici, Gian Gastone (see the painting above the door), and is named for the exhibits in the three cases known as scarabattole, ordered by Cosimo III to contain the ambers that belonged to his grandmother Maria Maddalena of Austria. The decoration of the scarabattole, including shells and moors' heads, alludes to the marine origins of amber and the African origins of ivory. On the wall, note the magnificent silver frame of Francesco Solimena's *St Anne and the Virgin* and an eighteenth-century Roman silver relief showing the *Deposition*. Also of interest is the table in pietre dure mosaic made by the Imperial workshops in Prague at the time of Rudolph II. The table, which shows an attractive landscape, rests on a base of gilded wood designed by the Dutch sculptor Vettore Crosten (1704), to whom the mirror is also attributed.

The SALA DEL CONSIGLIO PRIVATO (private council room) displays vases in pietre dure and rock-crystal from the sixteenth and seventeenth centuries; the consoles on which they stand are from the old Gem Cabinet of the Uffizi. The technique of pietre dure derived from the cult of the antique and the enthusiasm of Florentine Renaissance artists for the rare inlaid marble and stones of the 'opus sectile' of Imperial Rome. The Mannerist taste for precious materials and the technical ingenuity of Roman marble workers of the Middle Ages led to the art of the hard-stone mosaic, introduced to Florence in the sixteenth century by the architect Giovan Battista Dosio, who designed the fine table inlaid with white and black Aquitaine marble in the SALA DELLE COLONNE.

Although they were more difficult to cut than the marbles used in the Roman tradition, pietre dure (jasper, lapis lazuli, amethyst, onyx, agate) were soon adopted for Florentine mosaic-work, which became fashionable in the courts of Paris, Vienna and Madrid, where one can still see tables, cabinets and other objects made by the local factories.

It was the Grand Duke Francesco I who encouraged the use of precious stones and employed the Caroni brothers and Bernardino Gaffuri, specialists in rock-crystal and creators of fantastic zoomorphic vases first produced in the glassworks of the Casino di San Marco (now seat of the Florence Court of Appeal).

Among many outstanding crystals are the plate with Noah's Ark from the inheritance of Caterina de' Medici, wife of Henri II of France, the cup of Diane

Amber in the form of a heart. German manufacture

Inv. Bargello n.48

One of the ambers from the collection of Maria Maddelena of Austria, exhibited in 18th-century cases (scarabattole).

Lapis lazuli vase mounted in gold and gilt-copper, 1583

Height 40.5 cm
Inv. Gemme no. 802

Designed by Bernardo Buontalenti (Florence 1531–1608) – it was mounted by Jacques Bylivelt (Delft 1550–1603).

de Poitiers, mistress of Henri II, with their interlaced initials on its pierced gold cover, and the casket with panels showing scenes from the Life of Christ in finely worked rock-crystal inlay, backed by thin sheets of silver. The casket, executed by Valerio Belli, was given by Pope Clement VII to François I on the occasion of the marriage of Henri II to Caterina de' Medici, Clement's niece.

Many of these objects were executed by famous artists, such as the lapis lazuli *flask* with enamelled and gilded mounts in the form of harpies by the goldsmith Jacques Bylivelt, designed by the court architect and sculptor Bernardo Buontalenti, who also designed furniture and theatrical sets and costumes of great refinement. The small flights of stairs beneath the windows in the audience chambers are attributed to him.

On the mezzanine where the Grand Duke kept part of his treasury is the SALA DEI CAMMEI OVVERO DELLE PIETRE (room of the cameos or stones). Carnelian, agate and onyx were worked in relief with grinding wheels and abrasives made of sand or powdered diamond mixed with water. The cameos show a wide range of subjects, including portraits of the Medici. There are some famous objects in this room, such as the *gold oval bas-relief* with pietre dure mosaic showing the Piazza della Signoria and the equestrian statue of Cosimo I, or Giambologna's *seven gilded bas-reliefs* on backgrounds of pietre dure showing the *Deeds of Francesco I*. In the glass cases on the left wall are small vases in pietre dure from the Tribune of the Uffizi, a Mexican turquoise mask framed with gilded branches in allusion to the coat of arms of Vittoria della Rovere, and a panel of miniature mosaic, showing birds, made in Rome by Marcello Provenzale in 1615.

The SALA DEI GIOIELLI (jewel room) is devoted to the jewellery of Anna Maria Luisa, the Electress Palatine, the last of the Medici, whose portrait by Antonio Domenico Gabbiani shows her wearing a jewelled clasp. After the death of her brother, the Grand Duke Gian Gastone, she inherited the Medici collections, which included the jewellery that was taken to Vienna by Francis Stephen of Lorraine and restored to Italy after the first World War. Typical of the Electress Palatine's jewels is the Triton, a baroque pearl of the kind Flemish and Dutch goldsmiths mounted with precious stones and enamel to create extravagant animal forms and mythological figures. Unusual pieces include the Soldier and the Cobbler, the Knifegrinder and the Muleteer, German work of the late

Onyx cameo of Cosimo I and his family
Giovan Antonio de' Rossi (Milan 1517 – Rome post 1575)
Inv. Bargello no. 1

seventeenth century that anticipates the creations of eighteenth-century Meissen porcelain. In the same room is an ex-voto of *Cosimo II*, showing the Grand Duke kneeling before an altar, in pietre dure mosaic, gold, precious stones and enamel. In the glass case on the right there is an outstanding engraved carnelian with a profile of the Dominican martyr Girolamo Savonarola, carved between 1498 and 1516 by Giovanni delle Corniole.

The next rooms contain the Tesoro di Salisburgo (Salzburg treasure), which has been in Palazzo Pitti since the time of Ferdinand III of Lorraine. Returning to Florence from the exile imposed upon him by Napoleon, Ferdinand brought the silver of the prince-bishops of Wurzburg and Salzburg, in retaliation for Napoleon's appropriation of the masterpieces of Palazzo Pitti (returned after 1815). Note the double ostrich-egg chalice (ostrich egg was thought to give protection from poison) by German goldsmiths of the fourteenth century, and the eighteenth-century German portable altar in white and red coral, mother-of-pearl, tortoise-shell, gilded silver, cameos and precious stones.

The second room of the Tesoro has a large glass case along the wall with an amphora for pouring water into the mesciroba (ewer) for washing the hands at meals (as forks were not yet used in sixteenth-century Austria). Fifty-four silver-gilt cups or plates are decorated with various subjects, including the seasons, the elements, the months of the year, and the virtues. They bear the marks of two Augsburg goldsmiths, Paul Hubner and Cornelius Erb.

In the glass case to the left there are objects used at the Tuscan court, including the necessaire da viaggio (travelling case) of Ferdinand III of Lorraine, and the Neo-Classical vermeil table service used by Napoleon's sister Elisa Baciocchi for state dinners (other pieces are in the Quirinale Palace in Rome).

Paul Hubner. Plate in silver-gilt depicting Orpheus and the animals
German, 16th century, Salzburg treasure
Inv. A.s.e. no. 10

Triton
Enamelled gold, pearls, rubies, emeralds and garnets
Flemish 1580–90
80 x 54mm
Inv. Gemme no. 2495

**Pietra dure low relief of Piazza della Signoria by
Bernardino Gaffuri with gold mount by Jacques
Bylivelt**

Oval 25.5 x 18 cm
Inv. Gemme no. 823

**Rock-crystal vase in the shape of a bird with
gold mount. Sarachi workshop?, second half of
16th century**

Inv.Gemme no. 721

The vase, engraved with two hunting scenes, was made in
Milan in 1589 to celebrate the wedding of Ferdinando I with
Christine of Lorraine.

**Travelling case of Ferdinand III of Lorraine
containing French silver, 1769–89**

Inv. MPP no 8255

The LOGGETTA, which originally opened onto the Cortile della Fama, was frescoed in the early seventeenth century with grotesques and panels showing scenes of bronze-casting, the making of firearms and the discovery of America (with Columbus meeting a woman dressed in feathers sitting on a hammock), a man with a telescope and putti wearing spectacles (alluding to the inventions of Galileo). The lunettes above the doors are also frescoed, one with a cage full of animals and the other with monstrous birds presided over by an enormous owl. A large panel shows the Aztec emperor Moctezuma in a cloak and shield covered with feathers .

In the SALA DEGLI OGGETTI ESOTICI (exotic object room) the glass case nearest the door houses sacred vestments made of feathers and a Mexican jade mask of the seventh century BC. In the case on the right are painted precious shells with gilded silver mounts by northern European goldsmiths of the sixteenth century. In the case on the left-hand wall are grotesque and bizarre statuettes in the manner of Arcimboldo, made with shells imbedded in papier-mâché and dating from around 1600. These objects testify to the Medici family's contacts with the New World and elsewhere through their emissaries, ambassadors, merchants and missionaries.

The two SALE DELL'ESTREMO ORIENTE (Far Eastern rooms) exhibit objects from China and Japan. In the first room there is eighteenth-century porcelain of the Famille Blanc de Chine, white and blue, red, and green. On the wall opposite is the Kossu hanging given to Cosimo III in 1711 by Peter the Great, Tsar of Russia, which was restored in 1981. In the second room there is eighteenth-century Japanese Arita porcelain, which like the other porcelain came from the collection of Napoleon's wife Marie-Louise, Duchess of Parma and Piacenza. The plates in the central case are not porcelain but lacquer, a technique used in China since the fourth century BC in which tree sap is filtered through cloth, heated and mixed with dyes, and applied in layers.

The SALA DEI GIOELLI DEL XVII E XIX SECOLO (room of eighteenth- and nineteenth-century jewels) displays private donations, including an amethyst diadem by Cartier; a necklace of white gold and brilliants; parures in gold, enamel and coral; and miniature mosaics showing views of Rome, where this technique

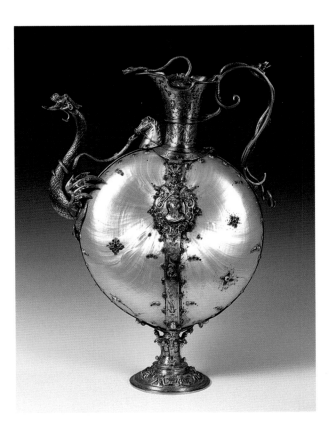

Mesciroba (ewer) made of two nautilus shells mounted with silver-gilt, rubies and turquoise
Flemish, 16th century

Height 30 cm
Inv.Bargello no.16

The mesciroba is mentioned in the collection of the Grand Duke Francesco I de' Medici in 1587 and later belonged to Cardinal Leopoldo. It is reproduced in the *Still-Life with Plates and Flowers* painted by Willem van Aelst for the Cardinal, which still hangs in the Palatine Gallery (Sala dei Putti Inv. no. 469).

was prized in the seventeenth century. Two other collections are interesting as reflections of eighteenth- and nineteenth-century taste, one of seals and one of small watches to be worn on ladies' belts or men's waistcoats.

The Palatine Gallery
LA GALLERIA PALATINA

One of the most outstanding collections of paintings in Italy and of great historical and artistic importance, the Galleria Palatina has a remarkable number of masterpieces by sixteenth- and seventeenth-century artists, including eleven works by Raphael, six by Fra Bartolomeo, seventeen by Andrea del Sarto, fourteen by Titian and ten by Rubens.

In contrast to the Uffizi, where paintings are hung according to chronology or school, in the Palatina they are hung in seventeenth-century fashion, covering the walls in an arrangement determined by aesthetic considerations alone. Their ornate frames carved with volutes, scrolls and exuberant festoons reflect the decorative motifs on the ceilings, giving a sense of organic harmony that was central to Baroque art. The importance of the frames in this aesthetic is indicated by the fact that some of the paintings were altered to fit them. For example, the Grand Prince Ferdinando had Rosso Fiorentino's *Madonna with Saints* in the Sala di Apollo enlarged to fill a larger frame, as we can see from the copy of the original now in Santo Spirito in Florence.

The statues, pietre dure tables, vases and other precious objects reflect Medici taste but also remind the visitor that this gallery, unlike most modern museums, was the home of ruling families for many years. As William Hazlitt remarked on his visit in 1826: 'the gallery's deep, mellow atmosphere of antiquity is for a connoisseur of painting like the patina of medals or the lees of wine for experts of a different type'.

The arrangement of paintings in the Palatine Gallery, filling the walls, is also found in other Italian collections for which works were accumulated over centuries, such as the Corsini Gallery in Florence and the Doria, Colonna and Spada collections in Rome. It is important to remember that the pictures and objects displayed in the Pitti were acquired as decoration for the private apartments of various members of the Medici family. Titian's portrait of the writer *Pietro Aretino* belonged to Cosimo I, Cosimo II owned Raphael's *Velata* (veiled lady), Caravaggio's *Sleeping Cupid* belonged to Cardinal Leopoldo and Titian's *La Bella* to Vittoria della Rovere, while Ferdinand III of Lorraine so admired his Madonna by Raphael that it came to be called the *Madonna del Granduca*. Ferdinand III and Leopold II of Lorraine completed the decoration of Sala dell'Iliade with frescoes by Luigi Sabatelli and the statue of Charity by Lorenzo Bartolini. Leopold II also redecorated the Sala di Prometeo according to nineteenth-century taste before the official opening of the Gallery in 1828. With this in mind, it is important for visitors to note the whole ambience of the Gallery, to appreciate the synthesis of the arts that makes it so fascinating.

Entering the first room in the Gallery, the ANTICAMERA DEGLI STAFFIERI (footmen's ante-chamber) we see images of the first and last of the Medici Grand Dukes: the bust of *Cosimo I* by Baccio Bandinelli and the portrait of *Gian Gastone* by Ferdinand Franz Richter. The decoration of the next room, the GALLERIA DELLE STATUE (statue gallery), executed in 1790 under Ferdinand III, reflects the Neo-Classical taste of the House of Lorraine. The room houses a series of Roman copies of Greek statues, mostly from the Villa Medici in Rome, and several paintings: *Naval Battle* by Willem van de Velde, the *Triumph of Galatea* by Luca Giordano, the *Tooth Extraction* attributed to Caravaggio and the *Entry of Christ into Jerusalem* by Jacopo Tintoretto.

Bust of Cosimo I by Baccio Bandinelli
Bronze

Sala di Venere: view of the room

Titian (Tiziano Vecellio)
(Pieve di Cadore 1490 – Venice 1576)
The Concert

Oil on canvas, 109 x 123 cm
Inv. 1912 no. 185

The painting was bought by Leopoldo de' Medici in Venice as a work by Giorgione, and it was only in the early twentieth century that art historians recognized the hand of the young Titian, especially in the central figure. The picture is thought to date to about 1510 when Titian was still strongly influenced by Giorgione, an influence most marked in the plumed figure on the left. The vitality of the central figure, sometimes identified with the musician Verdelot, who wrote madrigals, is typical of Titian. The intensity of the portrayal has inspired artists including Ingres, whose beautiful drawing of the work is in the Musée Ingres in Montauban. The painting also reflects the popularity of musical themes in Venetian painting (see *The Singing Lesson* by Giorgione in the Sala di Giove).

Passing through a room dominated by a large pietre dura Table of the Muses, made in Florence in the nineteenth century, we enter the SALA DI VENERE (Venus room), the first of the rooms overlooking the piazza, which was frescoed by the celebrated Baroque artist Pietro da Cortona from 1641–1647 and completed by his pupil Ciro Ferri from 1659–1665. Cortona's fresco cycle appears to follow a musical rhythm, from the andante section in the Sala di Venere, via the moderato of the Sala di Apollo and the allegro con brio of the Sala di Marte to the final slow movement of the Sala di Giove in which lovely maidens dance as though captivated by gentle melodies.

On the ceiling of the Sala di Venere, Venus is shown restraining a young man who is pulled by Pallas Athena towards Hercules, or glory, an allusion to the destiny awaiting the young Medici prince, Cosimo III. Hercules, both man and god, guides the prince's ascent to power. Celebrated figures from antiquity who renounced love for power are depicted in the lunettes, while stucco ovals contain portraits of the two Medici Popes, Leo X and Clement VII and of all the Grand Dukes from Cosimo I to Cosimo III as a child. In the left-hand lunette, above the entrance, there is a small grilled opening used for spying on guests of the Grand Duke.

At the centre of the Sala di Venere is Antonio Canova's marble statue of *Venus*. The room contains four masterpieces by Titian, *La Bella* (the beauty), *Il Concerto* (the concert) and portraits of *Pietro Aretino* and *Pope Julius II*; two landscapes by Rubens and two by Salvator Rosa, the portrait of *Baccio Valori* by Sebastiano del Piombo, two versions of *Apollo Flaying Marsyas*, by Guercino and Giovanni Bilivert, and *Christ Appearing to St Peter* by Cigoli (Ludovico Cardi).

Antonio Canova (Possagno, Treviso 1757 – Venice 1822)
Venus (Venere Italica)
Carrara marble, height 170 cm
Inv. sculp. no. 878

Canova's statue of *Venus* stands in the centre of the Sala di Venere. Sculpted in 1810, it was commissioned to replace the Medici *Venus* from the Tribune of the Uffizi, which was taken by the French during the Napoleonic wars. Like his *Three Graces* and *Cupid and Psyche*, it reflects Canova's ideal of female beauty, personified by Paolina Borghese in the *Venus* in the Borghese Museum in Rome.

Titian (Tiziano Vecellio)
(Pieve di Cadore 1490 – Venice 1576)
La Bella (1536)

Oil on canvas, 89 x 75 cm.
Inv. 1912 no. 18

The identity of this beauty has long been debated. The suggestion by Jacob Burkhardt that she was Eleonora Gonzaga, Duchess of Urbino, the wife of Francesco Maria della Rovere, was discredited by the publication of a letter of 1536 in which Francesco Maria refers to the subject as the 'woman in the blue dress'. She appears as the model for Titian's *Venus of Urbino* in the Uffizi, the *Woman in the Fur Coat* in Vienna and the *Woman with the Plumed Hat* in St Petersburg. Her identification with Isabella d'Este, the mother of Eleonora Gonzaga, also seems unlikely given the lack of resemblance to the portrait drawing attributed to Leonardo in the Louvre. Whatever her identity, the portrait is a marvellous depiction of dress in the 1530s, when elaborate earrings and the intertwining of ribbons and jewels in the hair were fashionable. Her beautiful dress with its low neck and very full slashed sleeves is lavishly described.

Peter Paul Rubens (Siegen 1577 – Antwerp 1640)
Ulysses on the Island of the Phæacians

Oil on panel, 121 x 194 cm
Inv. 1912 no. 9

Both this painting and the companion work, *Peasants Returning from the Fields*, belonged to the Duke of Richelieu and were brought to Florence in 1765 from the Imperial collections in Vienna. The warm evening light floods the landscape, and the panoramic view anticipates the modern cinema.

Salvator Rosa (Naples 1615 – Rome 1673)
Harbour with a Lighthouse

Oil on canvas, 393 x 234 cm
Inv. 1912 no. 15

This work, together with the companion piece on the opposite wall, was painted in about 1640 during the Neapolitan artist's stay in Florence. It was commissioned by Cardinal Giancarlo de' Medici, an enthusiastic collector of landscapes and still-lifes. The picturesque landscape bathed in golden light reflects the powerful influence of Claude Lorrain.

The decoration of the SALA DI APOLLO (Apollo room) shows Apollo as god of the arts and protector of the Muses (who are depicted in the spandrels). The young prince is presented to Apollo as he too is destined to become a patron of the arts, like the emperors and ancient rulers shown in the lunettes.

Here, in addition to Titian's striking portrait of the *Man with Grey Eyes* or *The Englishman*, are Tintoretto's portrait of *Vincenzo Zeno*, the *Cleopatra* by Guido Reni, the *Luco Lamentation* and the *Holy Family* by Andrea del Sarto and the *Madonna Enthroned with Saints* by Rosso Fiorentino. Also of interest is the *Accommodation of St Julian*, showing Christ pardoning Julian for mistakenly killing his parents, painted by Cristofano Allori, son of Alessandro Allori and pupil of Cigoli.

Tintoretto (Jacopo Robusti)
(Venice 1518-1594)
Vincenzo Zeno
Oil on canvas, 102 x 86 cm
Inv. 1912-13 Pitti

Titian (Tiziano Vecellio)
(Pieve di Cadore 1490 – Venice 1576)
The Man with Grey Eyes or *The Englishman*
Oil on canvas, 113 x 96 cm
Inv. 1912 no.92

Guido Reni (Bologna 1575–1642)
Cleopatra
Oil on canvas, 122 x 96 cm
Inv. 1912 no. 270

Andrea del Sarto (Florence 1486–1530)
The Luco Lamentation
Oil on panel, 238 x 198 cm
Inv. 1912 no. 58

The altarpiece was painted in 1523 for the church at Luco in the Mugello where Andrea del Sarto had fled with his family from the plague in Florence. His wife, Lucrezia, is portrayed as the Virgin, while his sister and step-daughter are depicted as the Holy Women.

The *Lamentation* shows Sarto's debt to his master, Fra Bartolomeo. The influence of the mature Raphael is reflected in the figures of the two Saints and that of Michelangelo in the composition, but the warmth and sympathy of the painting are peculiar to Sarto.

Rosso Fiorentino (Florence 1495 – Fontainebleau 1540)
Madonna and Child Enthroned with Saints
Oil on panel, 350 x 259 cm
Inv. 1912 no. 237

The painting is signed and dated 1522. Surrounding the Madonna and Child are St Peter, St Paul and in the foreground St Sebastian, St Bernard, St James, St Augustine and St Catherine of Alexandria, in the bright red robe. It was originally in the church of Santo Spirito, where it replaced the unfinished *Madonna del Baldacchino* by Raphael (now in the Sala di Saturno). At the end of the seventeenth century it was moved to Palazzo Pitti by the Grand Prince Ferdinando de' Medici, who had it enlarged to fit its present frame. This is the most striking instance of the importance of large frames in the Late-Baroque aesthetics of display, so clearly documented in the gallery.

In comparison with the Raphael altarpiece, Rosso Fiorentino's composition is crowded and more lively. It has the intense, shot colours typical of Rosso and Jacopo Pontormo, who were followers of Michelangelo and the foremost representatives of Mannerism in Florence.

The SALA DI MARTE (Mars room) is a complete expression of Baroque taste: the themes represented on the ceiling by the naval battle led by the young prince and Hercules triumphant with the spoils of war are echoed in Rubens' painting of the *Consequences of War*. The ceiling, the paintings, the consoles and the elaborate frames all express the rhythm, colour and movement essential to Baroque art which, according to the art historian Heinrich Wöfflin, is characterized by free forms.

The Sala contains two other works by Rubens, the *Four Philosophers* and the *Portrait of a Man*, the latter in a particularly fine frame. The portrait of *Cardinal Guido Bentivoglio* by Rubens' pupil Anthony Van Dyck can be compared with Titian's portrait of *Cardinal Ippolito de' Medici*, showing the son of Giuliano di Nemours in 'Hungarian' costume. Paintings by Venetian artists include Tintoretto's portrait of *Alvise Cornaro* and Paolo Veronese's *Portrait of a Man*. Two paintings by the Spanish artist Bartolome Esteban Murillo, the *Madonna of the Rosary* and the *Madonna and Child*, were acquired in the nineteenth century. Paintings of the *Penitent Magdalen* and the *Sacrifice of Isaac* by the Florentine artist Cigoli are typical of his style, which reflects the influence of Venetian painting and of late sixteenth-century Mannerism.

Peter Paul Rubens (Siegen 1577 – Antwerp 1640)
The Four Philosophers
Oil on canvas, 164 x 139 cm
Inv. 1912 no. 85

View of the Sala di Marte showing the ceiling

Anthony Van Dyck (Antwerp 1599 – London 1641)
Cardinal Guido Bentivoglio
Oil on canvas, 195 x 147 cm
Inv. 1912 no. 82

The subject is identified as a cardinal by his crimson robes, and his fine white surplice trimmed with lace is depicted in minute detail as was only possible for a Flemish painter of Van Dyck's skill. Bentivoglio, author of an account of the revolt of the Netherlands, was a friend of Van Dyck and his guest in 1623 when this portrait was painted. According to an anonymous contemporary biographer, this was considered the finest of Van Dyck's portraits, and all Rome flocked to see it.

Peter Paul Rubens (Siegen 1577 – Antwerp 1640)
The Consequences of War

Oil on canvas, 206 x 345 cm
Inv. 1912 no. 86

Painted in 1638, while Europe was still torn by the Thirty
Years War, the work depicts Mars leaving Venus to go to war,
while Europa raises her arms in desperation to the heavens
and the figures of Charity, Harmony and Art are trampled as
the winged Fury leads Mars away preceded by Hunger and
Pestilence. The painting embodies the idea of unfettered
form, which, according to Heinrich Wöfflin, was essential to
Baroque art as it replaced the restrictions of Renaissance
symmetry with new explorations of spatial concepts and sub-
stituted purity and transparency of colour with shadow and
atmospheric depth.

Paolo Veronese (Verona 1528 – Venice 1588)
Portrait of a Man
Oil on canvas, 140 x 107 cm
Inv. 1912 no. 216

The identity of this figure in the fur-lined coat is unknown.
A letter from the mid-seventeenth century to Cardinal
Leopoldo de' Medici, who had the painting purchased in
Venice, indicates that even then his identity was debated. He
is sometimes thought to be Daniele Barbaro, the author of
many treatises. The frame, made expressly for the portrait,
together with the finest of the Baroque frames in the Palatine
Gallery, was commissioned by Cardinal Leopoldo. The
painting can be dated to about 1560 and is executed in the
grandiose and free style fashionable in the late sixteenth
century.

Tintoretto (Jacopo Robusti)
(Venice 1518–1594)
Alvise Cornaro
Oil on canvas, 113 x 85 cm
Inv. 1912 no. 83

Tintoretto's aptitude for psychological penetration is revealed
in this portrait of the Venetian patrician, who was the author
of a treatise on sober living, a collector and patron of the arts.
Painted here just a few years before his death at the age of
98 in 1566, he appears to have reaped the benefits of his
own precepts for healthy living, and his gaze suggests calm
resignation and a certain stoicism.

The decoration of the SALA DI GIOVE (Jupiter room), once the throne room, shows Jupiter surrounded by Virtues crowning the prince, accompanied by Victory as the founder of Peace. This theme is also taken up in the scenes in the lunettes, which depict the gods who preferred peace to war: Vulcan, Apollo, Diana, Minerva and Mercury. The musical quality of the composition is enhanced by the dancing figures of the superb stucco work, also designed by Pietro da Cortona, a sumptuous frame for a precious jewel.

In addition to Raphael's *La Velata*, Titian's *Mary Magdalen*, Fra Bartolomeo's *Lamentation*, and *The Three Ages of Man* by Giorgione, the room houses two masterpieces by Andrea del Sarto: the *Annunciation*, reflecting influence of the Roman paintings of Raphael and Michelangelo; and the *St John the Baptist*, which presages the work of his famous pupil, Pontormo. Here too are Bronzino's portrait of *Guidobaldo della Rovere*, in which the armour is particularly beautifully painted, and the *Ecstasy of St Margaret of Cortona* by Giovanni Lanfranco of Parma.

Raphael (Raffaello Sanzio)
(Urbino 1483 – Rome 1520)
La Velata (The Veiled Woman)

Oil on canvas, 85 x 64 cm
Inv. 1912 no. 245

Considered one of the finest paintings in the Palatine Gallery, it is evocative of a myth: according to romantic tradition, the model, La Fornarina, the daughter of a Roman baker, inspired Raphael's passion to such an extent that he neglected work on the frescoes in the Villa Farnesina. Whatever her identity, she is clearly the same model, although idealized, portrayed in the *Sistine Madonna* and the *Madonna della Seggiola*. The painting is of exceptional pictorial quality, as described by Marco Chiarini: 'the quiet chromatic range is highlighted by the warmth of her gaze and her living, palpable flesh: the puffed sleeve is a marvellous pictorial passage painted in harmonious juxtapositions of white on white, which only Titian could have rivalled'. The picture was executed in 1515, about a year before Raphael's portrait of *Baldassare Castiglione* in the Louvre.

Giorgione (Castelfranco Veneto 1477/78 – Venice 1510)
The Three Ages of Man or *The Singing Lesson*

Oil on panel, 62 x 77 cm
Inv. 1912 no. 110

The 1987 restoration firmly established the attribution of this work to the young Giorgione, to circa 1500, when he was still fascinated by the shading effects of Leonardo (see the fine face of the old man) and attracted to allegorical compositions; the painting's title *The Three Ages of Man* is explained by the figures representing youth, maturity and old age. Previously attributed to Giovanni Bellini and Lorenzo Lotto, the painting is imbued with all the fascination and mystery characteristic of Giorgione's work. The possibility should not be excluded that it represents a *Singing Lesson* to be viewed alongside Titian's *Concert*.

Fra Bartolomeo (Florence 1472–1517)
Lamentation

Oil on panel, 158 x 199 cm
Inv. 1912 no. 64

During the restoration of the painting in 1988 two saints, St Peter and St Paul, were discovered under a layer of black paint, probably applied in 1619 to concentrate attention on the pathos of the central group when the altarpiece was bought by Cardinal Carlo de' Medici. It was at this time that the top of the painting was trimmed to adapt it to a frame in the cardinal's private apartments. The purity of design and the emotional composure of the figures had considerable impact on the Florentine school and clearly anticipate Andrea del Sarto's treatment of the same subject for the church at Luco in Mugello (now hanging in the Sala di Apollo).

Andrea del Sarto (Florence 1486–1530)
St John the Baptist

Oil on canvas, 94 x 68 cm
Inv. 1912 no. 272

Agnolo Bronzino (Florence 1503–1572)
Guidobaldo della Rovere

Oil on panel, 114 x 86 cm
Inv. 1912 no. 149

Table in Pietre Dure

The table has two almost identical panels, each decorated
with ears of corn, vine leaves and bunches of grapes trailing
around an amphora. It was designed by Jacopo Ligozzi for the
Opificio Fiorentino delle Pietre Dure, the Florentine factory
that still specializes in the creation of pictures and objects
in precious and semi-precious stones and now houses a
marvellous collection in its renovated museum.

Titian (Tiziano Vecellio)
(Pieve di Cadore 1490 – Venice 1576)
Mary Magdalen

Oil on panel, 84 x 69 cm
Inv. 1912 no. 67

'A magnificent lioness with an auburn mane', as the French
nineteenth-century traveller, Louise Colet, described the
Magdalen, and certainly the colour of her hair has long been
associated with Titian's name.

The wonderful treatment of the subject makes this one of the
masterpieces of Titian's early maturity, signed and datable to
c.1531, and it became one of the most popular iconographic
models of the penitent saint, despite the rather voluptuous
rendering of the model. It has, however, been noted that
nudity had symbolic meaning, representing Truth and
Penitence before God. This perhaps explains Cardinal
Borromeo's acceptance of the work, while others preferred
Titian's clothed *Magdalen* in the two versions in the
Hermitage, St Petersburg, and the Capodimonte Museum
in Naples.

The SALA DI SATURNO (Saturn room), frescoed by Pietro da Cortona's pupil Cirro Ferri, celebrates the apotheosis of the prince, now an old man, who is brought before Saturn by Prudence and Mars, to be crowned by Glory and Eternity. Hercules, the personification of the prince, mounts the pyre of immortality.

Paintings displayed here include a *Lamentation* by Perugino and various works by his pupil, Raphael. The portrait of *Tommaso Inghirami* shows Raphael's audacious use of red, also apparent in the portrait of *Leo X* in the Uffizi. The *Madonna del Granduca*, a favourite work of Grand Duke Ferdinand III of Lorraine, reveals the influence of Leonardo da Vinci in the use of shading and a simple dark background instead of the traditional interior view. Leonardo's influence is also apparent in his portrait of *Maddalena Strozzi Doni*. The tondo of the *Madonna della Seggiola* (Madonna of the Chair) is one of Raphael's best known paintings. The *Madonna del Baldacchino* (Madonna of the Canopy) was not completed, as Raphael left Florence for Rome, while the *Vision of Ezekiel* echoes the heroic quality of Michelangelo's paintings in the Sistine Chapel in Rome. Andrea del Sarto's *Dispute on the Trinity*, which was painted a year after Martin Luther's public criticism of the church, reflects the renewed interest in theological discussion. The Trinity is alluded to by the figure of St Augustine, author of the treatise De Trinitate. Also in the Sala di Saturno are Seabastiano del Piombo's *Martyrdom of St Agnes* and the *Infant St John the Baptist* by Carlo Dolci.

Raphael (Raffaello Sanzio)
(Urbino 1483 – Rome 1520)
Madonna del Granduca
Oil on panel 84 x 60 cm
Inv. 1912 no. 178

Raphael (Raffaello Sanzio)
(Urbino 1483 – Rome 1520)
Portrait of Maddalena Strozzi Doni
Oil on panel, 63 x 45 cm.

This portrait and the companion piece portraying Agnolo Doni was painted in about 1505 during Raphael's stay in Florence with the couple, to whom Michelangelo dedicated his famous tondo of the *Holy Family* in the Uffizi. The influence of Leonardo's recently painted Mona Lisa is evident in the pose and the position of her hands, although the landscape background lacks the mysterious quality of Leonardo's work. Raphael concentrates rather on the subject's material opulence and on her splendid pendant decorated with jewels signifying love, purity and fidelity.

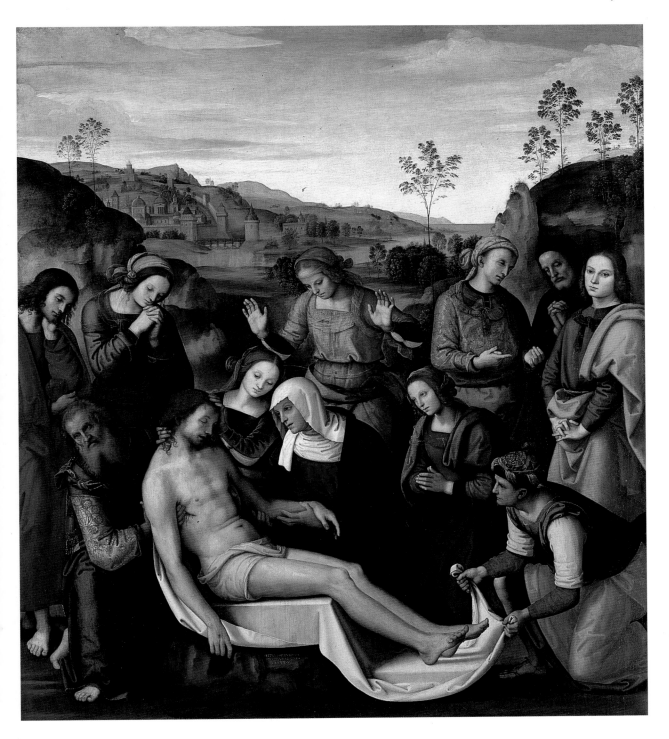

Perugino (Pietro Vanucci)
(Perugia 1445–1523)
Lamentation

Oil on panel 214 x 195 cm
Inv. 1912 no. 164

The altarpiece was painted in 1495 for the convent of the
Poor Clare nuns, but after the suppression of the order in the
Napoleonic period it was removed to the Accademia and then
to the Pitti. Typically, the scene is set in an Umbrian
landscape drenched in pale light, with the delicate trees that
reappear in Raphael's paintings.

Raphael (Raffaello Sanzio)
(Urbino 1483 – Rome 1520)
Madonna della Seggiola

Oil on panel, diam. 71 cm
Inv. 1912 no.151

The most celebrated of Raphael's Madonnas, this was among
the first paintings plundered by the French in 1799 to be
exhibited in the Louvre. While tradition has it that Raphael's
subject was a peasant girl, the painting was clearly an aristo-
cratic commission, perhaps from a member of the Papal court.
The Madonna is seated on a fine chair and wears an elegant
silk stole and turban, as was the fashion among gentlewomen
from the end of the fifteenth century. The work, which can be
dated to 1513, bears clear traces of the influence of Michelangelo in the perfectly balanced arrangement of form in the
traditional tondo. The splendid frame was probably designed
by Giovan Battista Foggini.

Carlo Dolci (Florence 1616–1686)
The Infant St John the Baptist Asleep

Oil on canvas, oval 45 x 58 cm
Inv. 1912 no.154

Sebastiano del Piombo (Sebastiano Luciani)
(Venice 1485 – Rome 1547)
The Martyrdom of St Agnes

Oil on panel, 127 x 178 cm
Inv. 1912 no. 179

The SALA DELL'ILIADE (Iliad room) was decorated between 1819 and 1825 by the Florentine Luigi Sabatelli with frescoes of the gods on Mt Olympus on the ceiling and scenes from Homer's Iliad in the lunettes. In the centre of the room is a marble statue of *Charity* by Lorenzo Bartolini, who trained in Paris under Jacques-Louis David and was also influenced by Jean-Auguste-Dominique Ingres and Antonio Canova. The most remarkable works in the room are two large altarpieces of the *Assumption* by Andrea del Sarto. The one on the right, executed between 1522 and 1525, was left unfinished, as is evident in the figure of the kneeling apostle. The composition of the one on the left, which is slightly later, 1526–27, is more advanced and shows the influence of Michelangelo and Fra Bartolomeo. The apostle in the centre of the painting is a self-portrait by Sarto, whose wife Lucrezia is shown as the Virgin. There is also a *Madonna and Child* by Sarto.

Notable among the portraits in this room is the splendid equestrian *Philip IV of Spain* by Diego Velazquez, *Eleonora de' Medici, Duchess of Mantua* by Franz Pourbus and *Waldemar Christian, Prince of Denmark* by Justus Sustermans. It is interesting to compare Ridolfo Ghirlandaio's portrait of a *Florentine Noble Woman* with the *Pregnant Woman* by Raphael. Here too is the large altarpiece of the *Virgin Appearing to St Philip Neri* by Carlo Maratta, the *Battle of Montemurlo* painted by the Venetian Battista Franco in celebration of Cosimo I's victory over the Florentine exiles, the *Baptism of Christ* by Paolo Veronese and *Christ in Glory with Saints* by Annibale Carracci. The gruesome depiction of *Judith and Holofernes* by Artemisia Gentileschi shows strong influence from Caravaggio.

Raphael (Raffaello Sanzio)
(Urbino 1483 – Rome 1520)
The Pregnant Woman (La Gravida)
Oil on panel, 66 x 52 cm
Inv. 1912 no.229

Diego Velazquez (Seville 1599 – Madrid 1660)
Philip IV of Spain on Horseback
Oil on canvas, 126 x 93 cm
Inv. 1912 no. 243

Artemisia Gentileschi (Rome 1597 – Naples 1652)
Judith and Holofernes

Oil on canvas, 117 x 93 cm
Inv. 1912 no. 398

It is interesting to compare this work with Cristofano Allori's painting of the same subject, in the next room. After denouncing the painter Agostino Tassi for rape, Gentileschi appears to have become morbidly attracted to the theme of Judith and Holofernes (there is another version in the Uffizi), identifying herself with the biblical heroine who wrecks punishment on the tyrant. She has clearly absorbed the innovations of Caravaggio's style.

Justus Sustermans (Antwerp 1598 – Florence 1681)
Waldemar Christian, Prince of Denmark

Oil on canvas, 70 x 54 cm
Inv. 1912 no. 189

Andrea del Sarto (Florence 1486–1530)
Madonna and Child

Oil on canvas, 87 x 65 cm
Inv. 1912 no. 476

Franz Pourbus (Antwerp 1545 – Paris 1622)
Eleanora de' Medici, Duchess of Mantua

Oil on canvas, 84 x 67 cm
Inv. 31 1912 – 391 Pitti

The SALA DELL'EDUCAZIONE DI GIOVE (the upbringing of Jupiter room) takes its name from the subject of the ceiling paintings, part of the decorations commissioned by Ferdinand III of Lorraine for the rooms of Napoleon I, which included the exquisite Neo-Classical bathroom by the architect Giuseppe Cacialli with bas reliefs by Luigi Pampaloni. Of special interest are the *Sleeping Cupid* by Caravaggio, inspired by a baby he saw in the street in Malta (note Cupid's bow and arrows in the frame) and *Judith and Holofernes* by Cristofano Allori in which the painter depicted himself as the victim of his cruel mistress Mazzfirra, who appears as the biblical heroine.

The SALA DELLA STUFA (stove room) once housed the heating pipes that warmed the adjacent bedroom of Cosimo III de' Medici. The walls are decorated with a cycle showing the *Four Ages of Man* painted by Pietro da Cortona between 1637 and 1640 as an allegory of the peace, work, war and violence which characterize human endeavour.

The Return of Ulysses painted on the ceiling of the SALA DI ULISSE (Ulysses room) alludes to the return of Ferdinand III of Lorraine from exile after the Napoleonic wars. Here, among other works, are Raphael's *Madonna dell' Impannata*, which takes its name from the cloth that covers the window in the background, the *Madonna and Saints* by Andrea del Sarto, a slightly later work than the *Dispute on the Trinity*, the *Death of Lucretia* by Filippino Lippi and Cigoli's *Ecce Homo*, as well as two fine portraits by Giovan Battista Moroni.

Caravaggio (Michelangelo Merisi da)
(Milan 1573 – Porto Ercole 1610)
Sleeping Cupid
Oil on canvas, 71 x 105 cm
Inv. 1912 no.183

Pietro da Cortona (Cortona 1596 – Rome 1669)
The Golden Age
Fresco, Sala della Stufa

Giovan Battista Moroni (Bergamo c.1525–1578)
Portrait of a Woman
Oil on canvas, 53 x 45 cm
Inv. 1912 no. 120

Cristofano Allori (Florence 1577–1621)
Judith and Holofernes
Oil on canvas, 139 x 116 cm
Inv. 1912 no. 96

Filippino Lippi (Prato 1457 – Florence 1504)
The Death of Lucretia
Oil on panel. 42 x 126 cm
Inv. 1912 no. 388

The SALA DI PROMETEO (Prometheus room) was frescoed in the early decades of the nineteenth century
and reflects the taste of Leopold II. During this period some of the Renaissance tondi (circular paintings),
of the Holy Family were given Neo-Classical frames,
with gilt rosettes. The most celebrated example is by
Filippo Lippi, showing two episodes from the life of
the Virgin behind seated figures of the Madonna and
Child. There are also two portraits by Sandro Botticelli, the *Holy Family with St Catherine* by Luca Signorelli, *Mary Magdalen* by Bachiacca and the *Adora-
tion of the Magi* and *The Eleven Thousand Martyrs* by
Pontormo, strongly influenced by Michelangelo.
Bachiacca's *Magdalen* is probably a portrait of the
Roman courtesan Pentesilea.

The console table showing Apollo and the Muses
was made in Florence in the 19th century.

Bachiacca (Francesco Ubertini)
(Florence 1494–1557)
Mary Magdalen
Oil on canvas, 51 x 42 cm
Inv. 1912–102

Luca Signorelli (Cortona c.1441–1523)
Holy Family with St Catherine
Oil on panel, diam. 99 cm
Inv. 1912 no. 355

Filippo Lippi (Florence 1406/7–1469)
Virgin and Child with Scenes from the Life of the Virgin
Oil on panel, diam. 135 cm
Inv. 1912 no 343

Guido Reni (Bologna 1572–1642)
The Young Bacchus

Oil on canvas, 87 x 70 cm
Inv. 1912 no. 102

An allegorical study of pleasure and earthly delight, this painting reflects the influence of the young Caravaggio on Reni, especially of the still-lifes such as the delightful *Basket of Fruit* in the Pinacoteca Ambrosiana in Milan, from which Reni appears to have borrowed the vine leaves to adorn his young Bacchus.

Pontormo (Jacopo Carucci)
(Empoli 1494 – Florence 1557)
The Eleven Thousand Martyrs

Oil on panel, 73 x 67 cm
Inv. 1912 no. 182

The CORRIDOIO DELLE COLONNE (corridor of the columns) takes its name from the alabaster columns flanking the door. It houses a series of views and landscapes by Dutch and Flemish artists collected by Cosimo II and Cosimo III de' Medici, such as a *View of Rome* by Gaspar van Wittel and the *Discovery of Moses* by Cornelis van Poelenburgh. Other works include *The Mill* by Filippo Napoletano.

From the SALA DELLA GIUSTIZIA (Justice room), dedicated to sixteenth-century Venetian painting including Bonifacio de' Pitati's *The Emperor Augustus and the Tiburtine Sibyl* and Titian's marvellous portrait of *Tommaso Mosti*, we pass to the SALA DI FLORA (floral room), with Tuscan works, such as Alessandro Allori's

Filippo Napoletano (Naples? 1585/90 – Rome 1629)
The Mill

Oil on copper
30.5 x 23 cm
Inv. 1890 no. 1214

Console table in scagliola with Apollo and the Muses

Florentine work, late 18th century

Gaspar van Wittel
(Amersfoort 1652 – Rome 1725)
View of Rome

Gouache on parchment, 29 x 41 cm
Inv. 1890 no. 1247

Cornelis van Poelenburgh (Utrecht c.1586–1667)

The Discovery of Moses

45 x 63 cm
Inv. 1890 no. 1203

Madonna and Child and two paintings by Andrea del Sarto of *Stories from the Life of Joseph* and then into the SALA DEI PUTTI (cupids room), displaying Northern paintings, like the beautiful *Still-Life* by Rachel Ruysch and Rubens' grisaille (monochrome) painting of the *Three Graces*, a seascape by Ludolph Backhuysen and the charming *Girl with a Candle* by Gottfried Schalcken. All three rooms were decorated in the nineteenth century.

Bonifacio de' Pitati (Verona c.1487 – Venice 1553)
The Emperor Augustus and the Tiburtine Sibyl
Oil on canvas, 105 x 124 cm
Inv. 1912 no. 257

Titian (Tiziano Vecellio)
(Pieve di Cadore 1490 – Venice 1576)
Tommaso Mosti (?)
Oil on canvas, 85 x 66 cm
Inv. 1912 no.495

Alessandro Allori (Florence 1535 – 1607)
Madonna and Child
Oil on canvas, 133 x 94 cm
Inv. 1912 no.442

Rachel Ruysch (Amsterdam 1664–1750)
Still Life with Fruit, Flowers and Insects
Oil on canvas, 89x 69 cm
Inv. 1912 no. 451

Ludolph Backhuysen (Emden 1631– Amsterdam 1708)
Ships at Sea
Oil on canvas, 65 x 79 cm
Inv. 1912 no. 464

Gottfried Schalcken (Made 1643 – L'Aja 1706)
Girl with a Candle

Oil on canvas, 61 x 50 cm
Inv. 1890 no. 1118

Returning to the SALA DI PROMETEO, we enter the GALLERIA DEL POCCETTI, named for Bernardino Poccetti who was thought to have executed the ceiling frescoes for Cosimo II de' Medici. (These were in fact painted by Matteo Rosselli and Filippo Tarchiani.) A porphyry bust of *Cosimo II* stands in the centre of the room. which was once an open loggia connecting the original nucleus of the Palace with the seventeenth-century additions. The painting of *Hyla and the Nymphs* is by Francesco Furini, the *Martyrdom of St Bartholomew* is by Jusepe de Ribera, Domenico Fetti painted the *Lost Drachma* and the *Portrait of a Young Man* is attributed to Pontormo. The pietre dure table in the corridor was designed by Giovan Battista Foggini.

Francesco Furini (Florence 1603–1646)
Hyla and the Nymphs
Oil on canvas, 230 x 261 cm
Inv. 1890 no. 3562

Jusepe de Ribera (Jativa de Valencia 1591 – Naples 1652)
Martyrdom of St Bartholomew

Oil on canvas, 146 x 216 cm
Inv. 1912 no. 19

Domenico Fetti (Rome c.1589 – Venice 1624)
The Lost Drachma

Oil on panel, 75 x 44 cm
Inv. 1912 no. 30

The SALA DEI TAMBURI (drums room), furnished with drum-shaped pieces in the Empire style, has a painted ceiling and monochrome frieze by Luigi Ademollo. Beyond it is the SALA DEL CASTAGNOLI with the marvellous nineteenth-century pietre dure Table of the Muses. This room leads into the QUARTIERE DEL VOLTERRANO (Volterrano apartments), once the private quarters of the Grand Duchess Vittoria della Rovere, to whom the ceiling fresco by Baldassare Franceschini, known as *Il Volterrano*, is dedicated. A typically Tuscan wit informs both Volterrano's painting the *Joke Played on the Priest Arlotto* and *Venus Combing Fleas from Cupid's Hair* by Giovanni da San Giovanni.

Pietre dure table designed by Giovan Battista Foggini, 1716

Volterrano (Baldassare Franceschini)
(Volterra 1611 – Florence 1689)
The Joke Played on the Priest Arlotto

Tempera on canvas, 107 x 150 cm
Inv. 1890 no. 582

The painting is typical of the light-hearted, even facetious Florentine spirit, which was evident as early as the fourteenth century in literature (the tales of Boccaccio) and reflected in the seventeenth century in the paintings of Giovanni da San Giovanni and Volterrano. Here we see the joke played on the priest Arlotto by his friends, who send him to get wine from the cellar while they make the most of his absence to taste his specially prepared food.

Giovanni da San Giovanni (Giovanni Mannozzi)
(San Giovanni Valdarno 1592 – Florence 1636)
Venus Combing Fleas from Cupid's hair

Oil on canvas, 229 x 173 cm
Inv. 1890 no. 212

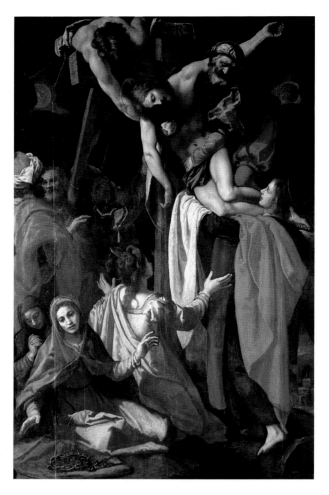

From the SALA DELLE ALLEGORIE (allegories room), dominated by the *Deposition* by Cigoli, through the SALA DELL'ARCA (Ark room) with a fresco by Luigi Ademollo of *David and the Ark of the Covenant*, we enter the SALETTA DELLE MINIATURE (miniatures room) with small works on parchment by Giovanna Garzoni.

Cigoli (Ludovico Cardi)
(San Miniato, Florence 1559 – Rome 1613)
Deposition
Oil on canvas, 321 x206 cm
Inv. dep. 51

Giovanna Garzoni (Ascoli Piceno 1600 – Rome 1670)
Grapes and Pears
Gouache on parchment, 39 x 49 cm
Inv. 1890 no. 4769

Much patronized by the Medici, Garzoni executed numerous miniatures on parchment for Cardinal Leopoldo, Grand Duke Ferdinando II and Cardinal Carlo. She delighted in the detailed description of flowers and fruit drawn from life, and this work shows that she was a worthy successor to Jacopo Ligozzi, who painted fine tempera studies of fruit and flowers for Francesco I de' Medici.

Giovanna Garzoni (Ascoli Piceno 1600 – Rome 1670)
Plate with Plums, Jasmine and Walnuts
Gouache on parchment, 24 x 35 cm
Inv. 1890 no. 4751

The last rooms are the SALA DI ERCOLE (Hercules room), with Neo-Classical frescoes by Pietro Benvenuti of *The Labours of Hercules*, the SALA DELL'AURORA (Aurora room), dominated by seventeenth-century Florentine paintings: *Jacob at the Well* by Lorenzo Lippi, *St Ivo Protector of the Young* by Jacopo da Empoli and *An Episode from Gerusalemme Liberata* by Jacopo Vignali. The SALA DI BERENICE (Berenice room) has a large altarpiece of the *Martyrdom of St Cecilia* by Orazio Riminaldi, *Adam and Eve* by Francesco Furini and *Joseph and Potiphar's Wife* by Giovanni Bilivert.

Last of all is the SALA DI PSICHE (Psyche room) with paintings by Salvator Rosa dating from his Florentine period, such as the *Landscape with Ruined Bridge*. Rosa was the most famous landscape painter of the seventeenth-century Neapolitan school, the creator of the 'picturesque' taste that became so popular in Italy and elsewhere.

Salvator Rosa (Naples 1615 – Rome 1673)
Landscape with Ruined Bridge
Oil on canvas, 106 x 127 cm
Inv. 1912 no. 306

The Royal Apartments
GLI APPARTAMENTI REALI

These rooms in particular demonstrate the evolution of taste over the centuries, from the late Baroque of the last Medici and the Rococo of the Lorraine dynasty to the Neo-Baroque and eclecticism of the House of Savoy.

The SALA DELLE NICCHIE (niches room) is where Cosimo I de' Medici created the first Florentine museum of antique sculpture, with statues from Rome (now divided between the Pitti and the Uffizi). The monochrome fresco decoration of the room was executed about 1791 by Giuseppe Maria Terreni for Ferdinando III of Lorraine, and copies of the statues were placed in the niches. Portraits of various members of the Medici family by Justus Sustermans are also displayed in this room.

The rooms leading off the SALA DELLE NICCHIE were occupied in the seventeenth century by Prince Carlo de' Medici and, towards the end of the century, by Grand Prince Ferdinando, who assembled a collection of Venetian paintings in the ALCOVA (now a chapel). Peter Leopold of Lorraine used these rooms as his private apartments, removing the paintings to the rooms that now form the Galleria Palatina. Two additions were made to the apartments, the SALOTTO OVALE (oval drawing room) and the SALOTTO TONDO (round drawing room), which became the private rooms of the Bourbon Grand Duchess Maria Luisa.

During the reign of the Savoy the rooms were taken over by Queen Margherita and King Umberto I, who celebrated their wedding here in May 1868.

An inventory drawn up in 1911 before the Palace became the property of the Italian State was used as a guide for the restoration of the apartments, which was completed in 1993. In addition to basic structural work, the furniture and wall fabrics in particular were restored to their original splendour and the carpets were returned after long years in storage.

It was because of their precious materials – dazzling silks, damasks and brocades – that in the eighteenth century these rooms came to be called the QUARTIERE DELLE STOFFE (the fabrics apartments), and each room is named after the fabric covering the walls.

The SALA VERDE (green room) is decorated and furnished in a Neo-Classical style with two consoles, vases and an Empire clock in addition to various

The Sala Verde

sixteenth- and seventeenth-century paintings including the *Knight of Malta* by Caravaggio.

The SALA ROSSA (red room), lined in crimson silk, has a fine carpet of mid-nineteenth century French manufacture. It was used by the Savoy as the throne room, although the king preferred the Villas of Poggio a Caiano and Petraia where he could indulge his great passion, hunting. Both the canopy above the throne and the Neo-Baroque mirror bear the Savoy coat of arms.

The SALA CELESTE (blue room), lined in nineteenth-century French silk, has an extremely fine chandelier decorated with fruit and flowers made in 1697 by the Dutch artist Vettorio Crosten. The walls are hung with portraits of the Medici family by Justus Sustermans.

The CAPPELLA (chapel) is a superb example of the Late-Baroque taste of the last Medici and in particular of the Grand Prince Ferdinando, who ordered the stuccoes and the carvings from the court sculptor Giovan Battista Foggini. Foggini was also responsible for the extraordinary pietre dure frame for the painting of the *Madonna and Child* by Carlo Dolci.

The SALA DEI PAPPAGALLI (parrots room) takes its name from the eagles, mistaken for parrots, on the Empire style wall-covering. The Empire clock originally bore a bust of Napoleon, but it was replaced in 1814 by one of Ferdinand III of Lorraine.

The SALOTTO GIALLO DELLA REGINA (Queen's yellow drawing room), once the private apartment of the Grand Duchess of Lorraine, was relined in the nineteenth century. The fine painting by Cornelis de Bailleur of *Ruben's Studio* is of particular interest, as is the nineteenth-century French gilt-bronze and porcelain candelabra and the French nineteenth-century porcelain brought from Parma.

The CAMERA DA LETTO DELLA REGINA MARGHERITA (Queen Margherita's bedroom) is lined in nineteenth-century French silk brocade. Its canopied bed, chaise-longue and nineteenth-century Chinese screen bear witness to the Queen's eclectic taste.

The SALOTTO OVALE (oval drawing room) reflects the Rococo taste of the Grand Duke Peter Leopold of Lorraine, who commissioned the room from Ignazio Pellegrini in 1763. The Grand Duke's love of Chi-

The Sala Rossa

The Salotto Ovale

noiserie is evident in the silk wall coverings, embroidered in Florence in 1780, the only eighteenth-century wall-coverings still in their original position. The Rococo consoles and embroidered armchairs are also beautiful.

The SALOTTO ROTONDO (round drawing room) was frescoed by Giuliano Traballesi, inspired by late-eighteenth-century classical models. The consoles and divans belong to this period, while the various small armchairs reflect the catholic taste of Queen Margherita.

The APPARTAMENTO DEL RE (king's apartment). Returning to the SALA DEI PAPPAGALLI we pass through the rooms which first Peter Leopold of Lorraine and later King Umberto I kept as their private apartments. The white and gold stucco ceiling dates from the time of the Lorraine, as does the beautifully restored bed with a canopy and the Savoy coat of arms. The Late-Baroque taste of the last of the Medici is evident in the prie-dieu and holy-water stoop, decorated in pietre dure by Foggini. Pietre dure work depicting the *Triumph of Europa* is also to be seen on the Empire side-table designed by Giuseppe Zocchi.

The STUDIO DEL RE (king's study) is lined in silk made in Florence in 1770. The French Louis XV desk and the Biedermeier cabinet came from the Ducal Palace in Parma, which was plundered by the Savoy to furnish the Pitti. (Note the bust of Umberto I's wife Margherita in the corner by the window).

The SALOTTO ROSSO (red drawing room) has crimson silk damask wall covering typical of Savoy taste, as are the mirror made by Mariano Coppedè in 1886 and the crimson velvet furniture bought by Victor Emmanuel II at the Italian Exhibition of 1861. The fine eighteenth-century Chinese vases were also from the Ducal Palace at Parma.

From the ANTICAMERA (antechamber), with eighteenth-century wall covering and paintings from the seventeenth and nineteenth centuries, we pass into the SALA DI BONA (Bona room), named after the fresco (c.1608–12) of the *Conquest of the City of Bona* in Tunisia by Bernardino Poccetti. A door in the wall on the right leads into the APPARTAMENTO DEGLI ARAZZI (tapestries apartment), which was known as the foreigners' apartment in the sixteenth century as it was where ambassadors were received. From 1589 the

most celebrated Florentine artists of the period worked on the decoration of the ceilings: Domenico Cresti, known as Passignano painted *Temperance* on the ceiling of the first and *Prudence* on the ceiling of the second room. Cristofano Allori painted *Hope* and Cigoli the allegory of *Charity* and *Justice* in the following two rooms. The rooms take their present name from the tapestries hung on the walls. Those depicting episodes fom the *Life of St John the Baptist* were inspired by Andrea del Sarto's frescoes in the cloister of the Scalzo convent in Florence; *The Young Gardeners* and *The Four Elements* were made at the Gobelins factory in France and *Water* or *Neptune* and *Fire* or *Vulcan* were made in the eighteenth-century in the Medici tapestry works.

In 1854 Pope Pius IX stayed in the SALA DELLA GIUSTIZIA (justice room), which was decorated for the occasion with superb eighteenth-century French furniture.

The closed loggia, the LOGGETTA DELL'ALLORI, frescoed with naturalistic motifs in 1587 by Alessandro Allori, is particularly charming.

Leaving the SALA DELLA GIUSTIZIA and retracing our steps through the two antechambers, we reach the SALA BIANCA (white ballroom) named for the fine eighteenth-century stucco work executed by the Albertolli brothers of Lugano for the Grand Duke Peter Leopold of Lorraine.

The Modern Art Gallery
LA GALLERIA D'ARTE MODERNA

In 1867, when Florence was the capital of Italy, King Victor Emmanuel II began to assemble a museum of modern art, with works he had acquired at the Universal Exhibitions added to those already collected by the Academy of Fine Arts, to the Martelli donation, and to the works acquired by the municipality of Florence. The MODERN ART GALLERY was officially opened in 1924, in the rooms left to the state by the House of Savoy. Most of the collection consisted of paintings by the Macchiaioli, nineteenth-century Italian painters, at that time regarded as 'modern'.

The gallery was rearranged in 1970, and its scope was extended to include works produced under the House of Lorraine and during the Napoleonic and Romantic periods. Works ranging in date from 1765 to 1915 are hung in groups according to their original collector. The arrangement of the gallery follows the same criteria as those of the other museums in Palazzo Pitti and is intended to reconstruct a nineteenth-century picture-gallery reflecting the taste of the Houses of Lorraine and Savoy, especially for Tuscan paintings.

As the number of works might be disconcerting for a new visitor, it is advisable to concentrate on the Macchiaioli. Masterpieces by these artists, the pride of the collection, are to be found in rooms 16, 17, 23 and 24.

Beyond the first room, dedicated to Neo-Classicism in Tuscany (paintings by Pompeo Batoni and a statue of *Psyche* by Pietro Tenerani), we pass into the SALA NAPOLEONICA presided over by a bust of *Napoleon* by the studio of Antonio Canova.

The rooms that follow are dedicated to history paintings (the *Entry of Charles VIII of France into Florence* by Giuseppe Bezzuoli), portraiture (*Alessandro Manzoni* by Nicola Cianfanelli, a self-portrait by Giovanni Fattori and a fine portrait of a *Noblewoman of the Morrocchi Family* by Antonio Puccinelli), and landscape (Serafino da Tivoli and Antonio Fontanesi). In ROOM 15 are paintings of peasant life by Cristiano Banti and of high society by Giovanni Boldini.

ROOM 16 is the first dedicated to the Macchiaioli, a group of artists who met regularly in the Caffè Michelangelo in Florence from 1855 and developed a new style in reaction to the academic tradition, painting as far as possible from actual experience. The

Silvestro Lega (Modigliana (Forlì) 1826 – Florence 1895)
Song of the Stornello (1867)
Oil on canvas, 158 x 98 cm
Inv. 1890-9807

This painter is associated with the Piagentina school, named after the green, almost rural area outside the walls of Florence where, from 1861, Lega and the other Macchiaioli, Borrani, Sernesi and Abbati began to sketch in the open air. Although Lega chose this direct approach, his training at the Accademia di Belle Arti was of fundamental importance in his subsequent development, like the purity of Ingres, which he expressed in his love of linear clarity. He was also attracted to the soft colours of the Tuscan primitives, revived with the nineteeth-century taste for intimacy.

Raffaello Sernesi (Florence 1838 – Bolzano 1866)
The Threshing Yard

Oil on panel, 19 x 51 cm
Signed in the lower left-hand corner
Inv. 82

In 1860 the Florentine painter began experimenting with painting 'sulla macchia', a technique based on patches of juxtaposed colour used to suggest forms in a synthetic way. This work was painted in 1865 while Sernesi was the guest of Diego Martelli, just one year before his death, fighting against the Austrians. The colours are applied in a close network of fine strokes and the layers of bright paint give the composition its luminous quality.

name 'macchiaiolo' was a pejorative reference to their application of colours in bold patches, without any attempt at shading or gradation of tone. The juxtaposition of different colours to create light and shade and the rejection of nuances of shading were considered as revolutionary in the nineteenth century as the work of the French Impressionists. The Macchiaioli's choice of subject matter was also innovative in its democratic bias, dealing with social observation, especially of the working and peasant classes. Giuseppe Abbati, Odoardo Borrani, Giovanni Fattori, Silvestro Lega, Raffaello Sernesi, and Telemaco Signorini were all friends of the writer Diego Martelli who formed a collection of their works at his house at Castiglioncello, near Livorno, a collection he left to the Modern Art Gallery. In ROOM 16, dedicated to the Martelli collection, note the paintings of the *House at Castiglioncello* by Giuseppe Abbati, *The Threshing Yard* by Raffaello Sernesi and *The Afternoon Rest* by Giovanni Fattori and compare them with the two Impressionist paintings by Camille Pissarro brought to Florence by Diego Martelli. Federico Zandomeneghi's two fine portraits of Martelli are in the same room.

ROOM 17 houses sculpture by the Tuscan Adriano Cecioni, including the *Visit to the Tomb*, *First Steps* and the *Child with a Cockerel*, as well as the small painting of the *Cloister of Santa Croce* by Giuseppe Abbati, to the left of the window. More than any other work, perhaps, it is the Macchiaioli manifesto. The group's interest in the portrayal of domestic intimacy is reflected in the *Song of the Stornello* and the *Visit to the Wet-nurse* by Silvestro Lega, the most important painter of the Piagentina school (named after the Florentine street where Lega lived).

In ROOM 18 are paintings commemorating the important events of the Risorgimento dominated by the *Italian Battlefield after the Battle of Magenta* by Giovanni Fattori, the leader of the Macchiaioli, who painted the site where the Italians won a battle in the second war of independence against the Austrians in 1859.

Beyond ROOMS 19, 20, 21 and 22, devoted to nineteenth-century historical paintings, with a pretty sixteenth-century ceiling and frieze, we reach ROOM 23, at the front of the palace, housing more Macchiaioli masterpieces such as the *Rotonda di Palmieri* by Giovanni Fattori, the *Portico* by Vito d'Ancona, and the *Staffato* (a man caught in a stirrup being dragged along by his horse), the portrait of his step-daughter and the *South-West Wind* or the *Libecciata*, all by Fattori. There are also some lively and realistic works by Telemaco Signorini: the *Roofs at Riomaggiore* and the *Prison Baths at Portoferraio*. The collection of Luigi Ambron, given to the Gallery in 1947, includes, in ROOM 24, several paintings by the Macchiaioli such as portrait of *Cousin Argia*, the portrait of his second wife, and *Diego Martelli on Horseback*, all by Giovanni Fattori; the *Window* by Giuseppe Abbati, paintings by Silvestro Lega, Telemaco Signorini and by the Neapolitans, Antonio Mancini, Filippo Palizzi and Vincenzo Caprile.

In ROOM 25 there are more works by Fattori inspired by the Maremma, the countryside around Grosseto, together with works by his followers such as Egisto Ferroni, Ruggero Focardi and Ruggero Panerai.

In the adjacent room there are further studies of farming life by Adolfo Tommasi, Eugenio Cecconi and Ludovico Tommasi.

Giuseppe Abbati (Naples 1836 – Florence 1868)
The Cloister of Santa Croce
Oil on cardboard, 19.3 x 25.2 cm
Signed in the lower left G.A. '43
Inv. 175

Abbati was among supporters of Garibaldi in the expedition to Aspromonte against the Bourbons in 1862, the year he painted this study. He described it as one of his first paintings using the 'macchia' technique, painting in bold patches of pure colour, which gave the group its name. It was painted during restoration work on the church, which offered dramatic contrasts of colour and light.

Giovanni Fattori (Livorno 1828 – Florence 1908)
Lo Staffato (Caught in the Stirrup) (1880)

Oil on canvas, 90 x 130 cm
Inv. 166

The painting, with all the elements of a cinematographic still, succeeds, with just a few quick strokes, in conveying the moment in which the rider is thrown from his galloping horse. An atmosphere of drama is evoked by the background colours.

Giovanni Fattori (Livorno 1828 – Florence 1908)
Rotonda di Palmieri

Oil on panel, 12 x 35 cm
Signed in the lower right: G. Fattori 1866
Inv. 220

Fattori, who was born in Livorno, studied at the Accademia in Florence and in 1859 began his first experiments with the 'macchia' technique. He continued working in this technique while staying at the house of his friend and patron Diego Martelli at Castiglioncello, making studies of peasant life in the fields. This work shows a family sitting under a canopy of the Rotonda dei Bagni di Palmieri, the then famous baths in Livorno. Painted on a narrow piece of wood (the Macchiaioli even painted on cigar boxes), it is considered the prototype of Macchiaioli painting. Composed in balanced layers of colour arranged with geometrical purity and tonal harmony, it is a masterpiece of its kind.

Giovanni Fattori (Livorno 1828 –
Florence 1908)
*La Libecciata (The South-West Wind)
(1880–85)*

Oil on panel, 28.5 x 68 cm
Signed in the lower left: Gio.Fattori
Inv. 221

The strength of the wind bending the tamerisk
trees on the beach powerfully expresses the
disillusionment of the artist's private and
political life, following the death of his wife
and the reactionary events in the 1880s.
A preparatory oil sketch for the painting
hangs nearby.

Telemaco Signorini (Florence 1835–1901)
Roofs at Riomaggiore

Oil on canvas, 56 x 80 cm
Inv. 277

One of the outstanding members of the
Macchiaoli group, Signorini was active in the
meetings at the Caffè Michelangelo and wrote
in defence of the new artistic trends. He
travelled to Paris, where he met Corot and
Degas, and to London where he exhibited his
studies of the coast at Riomaggiore. This small
village in the Cinque Terre on the Ligurian
Coast, with white-roofed houses clinging to the
cliffs and the green terraces descending to the
sea, provided inspiration for his 'macchia'
paintings on several occasions in 1881, 1887 and
again in 1892. This is perhaps one of his most
successful works.

Telemaco Signorini (Florence 1835–1901)
The Prison Baths at Portoferraio

Oil on canvas, 56 x 80 cm
Signed in the lower left T.Signorini
Inv. 283

This work, presented in 1901 at the VIII Biennale in Venice, reflects the extent to which Signorini was influenced by his Parisian sojourns and his adherence to the naturalistic poetic style inspired by Emile Zola, which was reflected in an interest in realism in both Italian literature and painting. Signorini visited the prison at Portoferraio on Elba in 1888 when he made a number of sketches of the inmates, revealing his compassion for the suffering of his fellow man.

Giuseppe Abbati (Naples 1836 – Florence 1868)
The Window

Oil on panel, 27 x 16.5 cm
Inv. 36

Filippo Palizzi (Chieti 1818 – Naples 1899)
Urchins

Oil on canvas, 35 x 50 cm
Inv. no. cap. gen. – 105

Antonio Mancini (Rome 1852– 1930)
Portrait of a Girl

Oil on canvas
43 x 33.5 cm
Inv. 1951

Plinio Nomellini (Livorno 1860 – Florence 1943)
Small Bacchus
Oil on canvas, 120 x 95 cm
Inv. no. cap. gen. – 451

ROOM 27 is devoted to Neapolitan views and landscapes including the *View of Capri* by Marco de Gregorio, and two paintings of the same subject, the *Shower of Ashes*, by Giuseppe de Nittis and Gioachino Toma.

ROOM 28 houses paintings by Italian and foreign Decadent artists, such as three panels, *Peace*, *Faith* and *Indolence*, by Galileo Chini inspired by the Orient, while in ROOM 29 there are three paintings, including the *Small Bacchus*, by Plinio Nomellini, prominent in the Divisionist movement, together with the Impressionist sculpture of Medardo Rosso, such as *Man Reading*.

Of especial interest in ROOM 30 are the intimate family paintings of Elizabeth Chaplin, the French painter who lived in Fiesole, and several works by Armando Spadini, Mario Puccini and Oscar Ghiglia who all worked in Florence in the early years of this century. Works by other celebrated Italian painters such as Giorgio de Chirico, Alberto Savinio, Gino Severini, Filippo de Pisis and Carlo Carrà will in future be exhibited in the MEZZANINO DEGLI OCCHI, above the Modern Art Gallery, to be dedicated to twentieth-century artists.

Galileo Chini (Florence 1873– Lido di Camaiore 1956)
Faith

Oil on canvas
200 x 126 cm
Inv. 442

One of three panels epitomising Chini's symbolist style, this was painted in 1912 during his stay in Siam, where he decorated the Royal Palace in Bangkok. The works he exhibited at the Venice Biennale in 1909 already reflected an interest in Japanese art and symbolism, then fashionable in Europe. He also worked in ceramics and as a stage designer.

Medardo Rosso (Turin 1858 – Milan 1928)
Man Reading

Bronze, height 41 cm
Inv. no. 659

Rosso trained in Milan with the painters of the Lombard 'scapigliatura' group, Daniele Ranzoni and Tranquillo Cremona, who reacted against the academic trend and advocated direct 'study from life', in which objectivity and subjectivity were blended to convey both the physical and psychological nature of the subject. Rosso regarded wax as the ideal means of achieving the required expressive quality, but he also worked in unpolished bronze to great effect.

The Porcelain Museum

IL MUSEO DELLE PORCELLANE

The elegant Palazzina designed by Giuseppe del Rosso and built in 1790 replaced the small Medici casino where Leopoldo de' Medici presided over meetings of the scientific academy 'del Cimento' and the young Gian Gastone had French lessons. Since 1973 it has housed the porcelain collections of the Medici, the Lorraine, Elisa Baciocchi, Maria Louisa Bourbon and the Savoy family.

The first room, which is devoted to French and Italian Porcelain, includes the remarkable series of biscuit statuettes showing various traditional Neopolitan costumes. These were made in the Royal Factory of Capodimonte in 1784 by Filippo Tagiolini, who introduced the biscuit technique to Naples after a period in Vienna. Tagliolini executed the amusing group called the *School of Bears*.

During the Napoleonic period Jean Poulard Prad was in charge of the Neapolitan factory when the cup with a Portrait of Caroline Bonaparte, wife of Joachim Murat, King of Naples, was made.

The production of Doccia porcelain was begun in Florence by Carlo Ginori in 1737, the year of Gian Gastone's death, and encouraged to expand by Peter Leopold of Lorraine and his successors. It was originally characterized by blue and white decoration and small bunches of flowers or tulip motifs, as we can see in the vases and Florentine services on display.

Blue was the predominant colour in the porcelain produced at the factory of Vincennes, founded in 1740 and transferred in 1756 to Sèvres (see the large Sèvres flower vase in lapis lazuli blue). Pastel colours with gilt decoration were also favoured for services, often combined with prints after François Boucher.

There are also some fine raised oyster dishes decorated with blue borders and small bunches of flowers from the Sèvres factory.

In the two central cases is Elisa Baciocchi's service, a present from her brother Napoleon in 1810. One part of the service was designed for the entrée, the other for the dessert.

Ferdinand III of Lorraine, uncle of Marie Louise, wife of Napoleon, was presented with the Sèvres porcelain portrait of Napoleon when he attended the christening of Napoleon's son, the King of Rome. The portrait is taken from the Emperor's portrait by François Gérard, now at Versailles.

Doccia: Cup with a view of the Rondò at the Pitti Palace

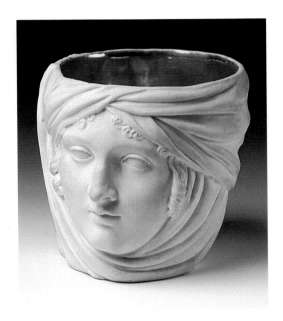

Poulard Prad: Cup with a portrait of Caroline Murat. Royal Factory, Naples, c.1810

Biscuit figure in a costume from the Kingdom of Naples, attributed to Filippo Tagliolini. Royal Factory, Naples, c.1785

In ROOM II Viennese Porcelain is displayed including the group depicting Maria Teresa of Austria and her son Peter Leopold. There is also a fine Neo-Classical service with views of Vienna taken from prints published by Artaria, collected by the Lorraine in Vienna and then brought to Florence to decorate the Medici Villas.

ROOM III houses Meissen porcelain and pieces from Nymphenburg, Frankental and Worcester, all taken from the Ducal Palace at Parma.

Meissen was the first porcelain factory to open in Europe, inaugurated in 1710 by Augustus II of Saxony. The marriage between his daughter Maria Amelia and Gian Gastone de' Medici fired the Grand Duke with enthusiasm for the ware, and the two tortoise-shaped sugar bowls and the hen tea-pot were part of his personal collection. Chinoiserie pieces, launched by Meissen, became popular throughout Europe, particularly in Naples, where there is a famous collection in the Capodimonte palace.

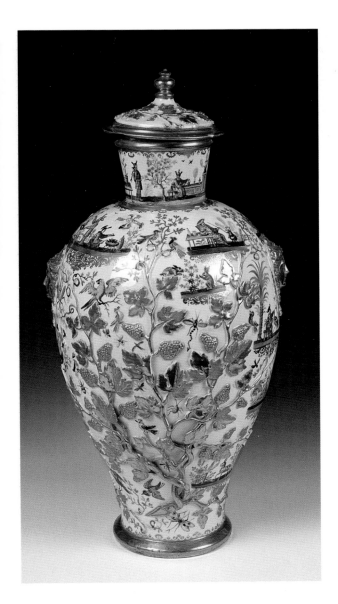

Meissen: Chinoiserie vase

Sèvres: Oyster stand

Evening dress, 'La Primavera' (spring). Rosa Geroni, Milan, 1905

The Costume Gallery

LA GALLERIA DEL COSTUME

Housed in part of the Palazzina della Meridiana facing the Boboli Garden, the Costume Gallery can be reached from the garden or through a corridor from the Modern Art Gallery. A sundial from the time of the Grand Prince Ferdinando gives the Meridiana its name. The Grand Prince commissioned the ceiling painting of an *Allegory of Time* by Antonio Domenico Gabbiani. The building was begun by Gaspare Maria Paoletti for Peter Leopold in 1776 and completed between 1822 and 1840 by Pasquale Poccianti, who added the ballroom and the rooms adjacent to the gardens of the Specola (observatory).

Both the Lorraine and the Savoy lived in these rooms, and they reflect particularly the taste of the Count of Turin and of King Umberto and Queen Maria José of Savoy, who lived here until 1946 when Italy became a republic.

The costumes on display reflect changes in fashion from the eighteenth to the twentieth century. Largely donated by individuals and groups, they are displayed in rotation for reasons of conservation. The paintings on the walls and ceilings are by nineteenth-century academic painters including Luigi Mussini, Annibale Gatti, Antonio Marini and Luigi Sabatelli.

Dress in silk velvet. Piedmont 1829

Man's suit. Italian, 1720–40

The Carriage Museum
IL MUSEO DELLE CARROZZE

The Carriage Museum, with carriages from the time of the Lorraine and the Savoy, is housed in the Rondò di Mezzogiorno.

The oldest example, dating from the mid-eighteenth century, is a coupé decorated with paintings of the four seasons. The sedan chair made for Maria Louisa Bourbon, daughter of Ferdinand IV of Bourbon and wife of Ferdinand III of Lorraine, is from 1793.

The finest carriage, built for Ferdinand III in 1818 after his return from exile during the Napoleonic wars, has recently been restored. The carriage, gilt with dragons and other motifs, is decorated with paintings by Antonio Marini depicting *Lorenzo the Magnificent and Poliziano*, *Cosimo I and Vasari*, *Cosimo II and Galileo* and *Ferdinand III in Glory* to show continuity between the two illustrious houses of the Medici and the Lorraine.

Other carriages awaiting restoration were commissioned in the nineteenth century by Ferdinand III of Lorraine for his son Leopold (the future Leopold II, Grand Duke of Tuscany).

There is a splendid carriage, originally belonging to Ferdinand II, King of Naples and then to Victor Emmanuel II of Savoy, who applied the Savoy coat of arms, together with allegorical references to Naples and Palermo, in embossed silver.

Fine equestrian equipment and watercolours of Victor Emmanuel II on horseback are also on display in the museum.

Carriage of Ferdinand II of Naples, later of Victor Emmanuel II of Savoy

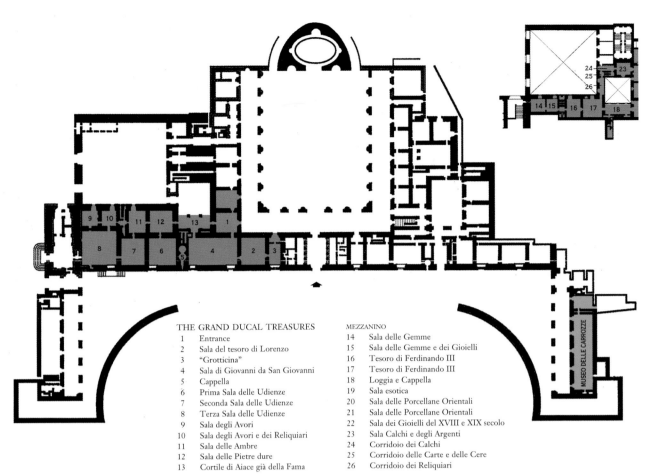

THE GRAND DUCAL TREASURES

1 Entrance
2 Sala del tesoro di Lorenzo
3 "Grotticina"
4 Sala di Giovanni da San Giovanni
5 Cappella
6 Prima Sala delle Udienze
7 Seconda Sala delle Udienze
8 Terza Sala delle Udienze
9 Sala degli Avori
10 Sala degli Avori e dei Reliquiari
11 Sala delle Ambre
12 Sala delle Pietre dure
13 Cortile di Aiace già della Fama

MEZZANINO

14 Sala delle Gemme
15 Sala delle Gemme e dei Gioielli
16 Tesoro di Ferdinando III
17 Tesoro di Ferdinando III
18 Loggia e Cappella
19 Sala esotica
20 Sala delle Porcellane Orientali
21 Sala delle Porcellane Orientali
22 Sala dei Gioielli del XVIII e XIX secolo
23 Sala Calchi e degli Argenti
24 Corridoio dei Calchi
25 Corridoio delle Carte e delle Cere
26 Corridoio dei Reliquiari

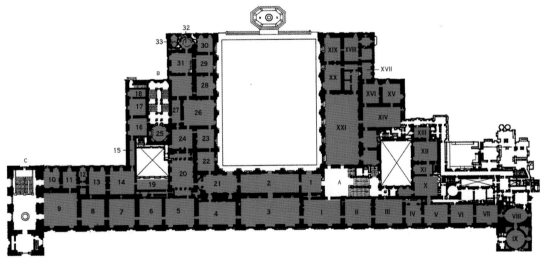

THE PALATINE GALLERY

1 Anticamera degli Staffieri
2 Galleria delle Statue
3 Sala delle Nicchie
4 Sala di Venere
5 Sala di Apollo
6 Sala di Marte
7 Sala di Giove
8 Sala di Saturno
9 Sala dell'Iliade
10 Sala delle Stufa
11 Sala dell'Educazione di Giove
12 Bagno di Napoleone
13 Sala di Ulisse
14 Sala di Prometeo
15 Corridoio delle Colonne

16 Sala della Giustizia
17 Sala di Flora
18 Sala dei Putti
19 Galleria del Poccetti
20 Sala della Musica
21 Sala del Castagnoli
22 Sala delle Allegorie
23 Sala delle Belle Arti
24 Sala dell'Arca
25 Cappella delle Reliquie
26 Sala di Ercole
27 Corridoio delle Miniature
28 Sala dell'Aurora
29 Sala di Berenice
30 Sala di Psiche

31 Sala della Fama
32 Vestibolo di Maria Luisa
33 Bagno di Maria Luisa

A Scalone dell'Ammannati
B Scalone Poccianti
C Scalone Del Moro

THE ROYAL APARTMENTS

I Sala Verde
II Sala del Trono
III Sala Celeste
IV Cappella
V Sala dei Pappagalli
VI Sala Gialla

VII Stanza da letto della Regina
VIII Gabinetto Ovale
IX Gabinetto Tondo
X Camera da letto del Re
XI Studio del Re
XII Salotto Rosso
XIII Salottino Giallo
XIV Sala di Bona
XV Sala della Temperanza
XVI Sala della Prudenza
XVII Loggetta dell'Allori
XVIII Sala della Giustizia
XIX Sala della Carità
XX Sala della Fede
XXI Sala Bianca

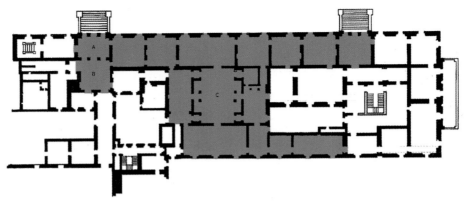

THE COSTUME GALLERY
A   Entrance
B   Sala della Meridiana
C   Sala da ballo

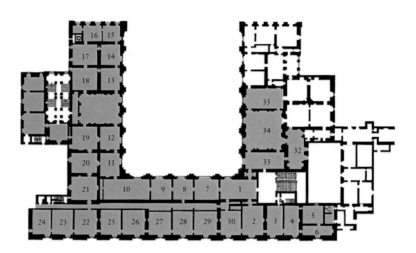

THE MODERN ART GALLERY
1   From Batoni to Neo-Classicism
2   The Arts during the Restoration
3   The poetic theme in Romantic art
4   The Purists
5   The historical novel
6   Landscape painting of the Sette and Ottocento
7   Neo-Classicism and France
8   Iconography of the Tuscan dynasties
9   The Demidoff and their world
10   The historical-allegorical theme between the Restoration and the Risorgimento
11   Stefano Ussi
12   Antonio Ciseri and Ottocento portraiture
13   Portraiture at the time of the Florentine capital
14   The mid-nineteenth-century landscape school
15   The Cristiano Banti Collection
16   The Diego Martelli Collection
17   Genre painting from the end of the Grand-Duchy and the Unification of Italy
18   The theme of patriotism
19   Antonio Ciseri
20   Stefano Ussi and the cultural climate at the time of the Universal Exposition
21   The celebration of the Risorgimento post Unification of Italy
22   Portraiture during the reign of Umbertina
23   The Macchiaioli
24   The Macchiaioli
25   The Macchiaioli, the post-Macchiaioli and rural life
26   Eugenio Cecconi: the countryside around Pisa and Livorno
27   Italian schools of the late nineteenth century. Italian painters abroad
28   Aspects of central European culture and Italian Decadence
29   Divisionism, Symbolism, social themes
30   The Secessionist movement and post-Impressionism in Tuscany
31   Sala delle Muse
32   Sala degli Staffieri
33   Sala da ballo
34   Sala della Musica

THE BOBOLI GARDEN

1   Grotta del Buontalenti
2   Grotticina di Madama
3   Anfiteatro
4   Café
5   Fontana del Nettuno
6   Museo delle Porcellane
7   Meridiana
8   Viottolone
9   Limonaia
10 Fontana dell'Oceano

FORTE DI
BELVEDERE

P.LE DI
PORTA ROMANA

PIAZZA PITTI

VIA ROMANA

Index

Page numbers in italics refer to illustrations